A History *of* Skiing *in* Colorado

by Abbott Fay

Western Reflections Inc.
Ouray, CO 81427

Revised Edition

Cover and text by SJS Design (Susan Smilanic)

Library of Congress Catalog Number: 99-64984
ISBN 1-890437-34-4

Western Reflections, Inc.
PO Box 710
Ouray, CO 81427
USA

Note: This is a revised, updated and expanded version of <u>Ski Tracks In The Rockies</u>: <u>A Century of Colorado Skiing</u> published in 1984.

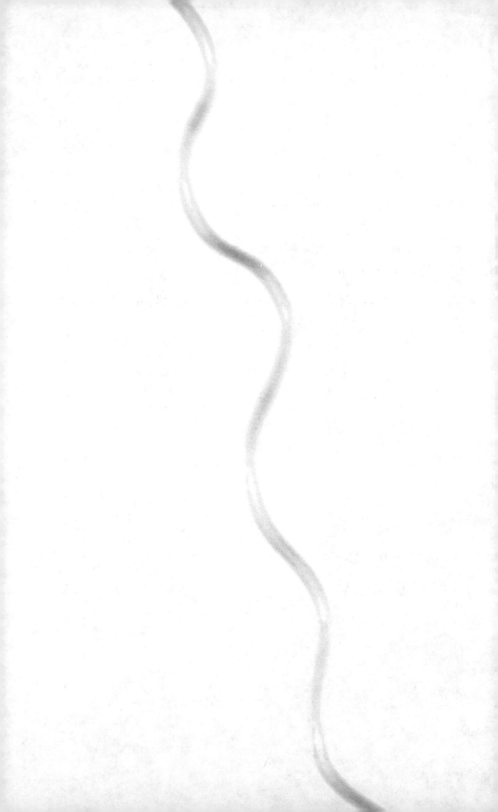

Table of Contents

Prologue   3

Chapter One: Breaking the Trail   7

Chapter Two: The Flying Norseman   21

Chapter Three: Arlbergs, Zipfelbergers and Eskimos   31

Chapter Four: Way Up Yonder in the Mountains   47

Chapter Five: Camp Hale, the Big Christy of Colorado Skiing   57

Chapter Six: Paepcke, Pfeifer and Powder   67

Chapter Seven: Prospecting the Powder   79

Chapter Eight: Learning How to Mine Snow   89

Chapter Nine: Slate Boards and Ski Wax   103

Chapter Ten: The Strange Case of the Almost Olympics   113

Chapter Eleven: Getting a Lift and Shooting Down Powder   123

Chapter Twelve: On Top of it All   133

Appendix I: Who Did What?   143

Appendix II: What Was Where?   165

Appendix III: What Was What?   171

Selected Bibliography   177

Acknowledgements   183

Index   185

Ski club at Irwin, 1883, when they called it a snowshoe club. This is believed to be the earliest documented Colorado recreational skiing organization.

Mellen of Gunnison photo.

Family ski fun in the nineteenth century.

Colorado Ski Museum/Hall of Fame photo.

PROLOGUE

While slaves pulled the massive stones up ramps to build the pyramids of Egypt, northern people, whose descendents would be Finns, Swedes, and Norwegians, skied on hunting expeditions. Scandinavians made their "snowshoes" by splitting wood into slats; the Norwegian word "skiboler" meaning, literally, two boards, and being the origin of the word "ski." Norse legends included a god and goddess of skiing, Ull and Skade, and it was the Viking ships which carried skiing to the far shores of the world.

Early references to what we call "skis" termed them Norwegian or Swedish snowshoes – not to be confused with the web snowshoes of recent use. Those early skis were not of matched length. A long ski served as a platform, a shorter one as sort of a rudder, and one long pole for control. The skis were made of rough wood, giving some traction, but they lacked grooves to prevent side-slipping.

Nordic migrants brought these "Norwegian snowshoes" to the mining camps of the New World and Australia during the nineteenth century. The first ski club in the world was founded at Kiandra, Australia, in 1851. Latter-day Vikings spread the ski gospel through the upper Midwest and out to the California gold camps where mail was skied across the high Sierras. While Frank Aubrey Bishop was the earliest recorded California skiing mail carrier, the most famous was John A. Thorenson, remembered in the lore of the Far West as "Snowshoe Thompson." These ventures led to sport skiing, and the nation's first competitive skiing club was founded at La Porte, California, in 1867. Racers waxed their boards with a mixture of tallow, beeswax, pine tar, and other "secret" ingredients, taking off on skis up to twelve feet long at speeds of up to ninety miles an hour!

There are all sorts of conflicting claims as to the earliest racing meets in this country. United States National Ski Association historians have held that the first ski meet was a jumping event at Red Wing, Minnesota, in 1887. On the other hand, *Outing* magazine for January of that year described downhill meets at Crested Butte and Gunnison, which had taken place the previous winter. Those races were among regular teams in the region, challenging the claim that the oldest ski team was the Aurora Ski Club of Red Wing, founded in 1886. There is no denial, however, that the vivacious Red Wing crowd set an organized pattern for racing. By 1891, there were so many ski clubs in the Great Lakes region that they formed a central organization at Ishpeming, Michigan. By 1904, this group evolved into the National Ski Association, and Ishpeming is deservedly the home of the National Ski Hall of Fame.

Canadians were early ski buffs, too. While Norway had led the way with its famed Holmenkollen meet, Canadian Ragner Omtvedt was jumping at Ottawa in the 1890s, soaring 203 feet to land on river ice, but breaking both of his ankles in the process! As the new century arrived, the first rope tow was built at Shawbridge, Quebec. By that time, skis were matched and grooved. Swiss and Austrians had taken up the sport and were schussing down the Alps, attracting world attention.

Hannes Schneider, from Arlberg, Austria, disdained his father's plans to turn him into a cheesemaker and invented the Arlberg system to replace the telemark turn. His basic turn, a snowplow and a half-snow-plow, or stem, was taught all over Europe.

New Englanders were also ski enthusiasts, forming the Nansen Ski Club at Berlin, New Hampshire. Dartmouth College staged the first winter carnival in 1911, and formed the first collegiate team in the early 1930s. By 1916, other colleges, including the University of Wisconsin and Western State College of Colorado, had skiing as regular features of their physical education programs.

Olympic skiing made its debut with the first winter games at Chamonix, France, in 1924. Anders Haugen, who, with his famous brother Lars, had been a Colorado champion, was the leader of the first American team. In 1932, the Olympics moved to Lake Placid, New York, pushing off an avalanche of skiing excitement in the United States. Lowell Thomas, who had grown up in Victor, Colorado, was the commentator who covered the event by radio and made the nation itch to feel the thrill of skiing.

Franconia, New Hampshire, was the site of the nation's first ski school, which opened in 1932. Two years later, ski buffs built the country's first rope tow on Gilbert's Hill at Woodstock, Vermont. By then skiers were using two poles and improved bindings. The Norheim heel binding made slalom races possible. The word "slalom" derived from the Norwegian word for "tracking down a smooth hill."

Blossoming out in the West were plans for large skiing resorts, including Sugar Bowl, California, and Alta, Utah. The resort which glamorized ski life the most was Sun Valley, Idaho. It opened with much fanfare in 1936. The inspiration of Union Pacific Railroad scion and later diplomat, Averell Harriman, Sun Valley attracted the elite of the era.

Colorado was making tracks in the Rockies, too. Its people were sliding down to Denver from mining camps on Loveland Pass, skiing mail over rugged passes, preaching sermons on circuit, tracking down stray cattle, and skiing just for the fun of it. A few were racing, and others were building the greatest of ski jumps.

Early snow tunnel across Main Street in Breckenridge, Colorado.

CHAPTER ONE
BREAKING THE TRAIL

He couldn't deny it any longer. Jim Baker was lost! One of the most famous of the doughty mountain guides, Baker was leading the Marcy expedition from Utah to Fort Massachusetts in southern Colorado during the "Mormon War" of 1857. Looking for Cochetopa Pass, east of present-day Gunnison, he had taken the wrong stream and now the hapless, starving party was knee-deep in snow. Undaunted, Baker carved out a pair of skis and scrambled up a nearby pinnacle to look for a landmark. Colonel Marcy noted this earliest provable use of skis in Colorado in his journal. The Marcy group eventually reached its destination, and Baker's use of skis indicates that probably scores of other trappers, guides, and traders had used them in the Colorado Rockies before that time.

With the gold rush of 1859, skiers swarmed over the mountains. Most of their skis were homemade from available wood, measuring from eight to twelve feet in length, five inches or so in width, and an inch thick. A simple thong held the ski to the foot – more extensive bindings were considered suicidal on such cumbersome boards. Sometimes a traveler would fasten a thong to the ski as a safety strap if the ski got loose. In manufacturing these crude models, steaming the tip into an upward curl was the hardest task the home craftsman had to face. Out in the snow, the skier used a pole, usually about eight feet long, to guide, brake, and balance. On steep slopes, he would often straddle the pole as a continuous brake.

Modern ski tourers might wonder about the uphill climbs with those primitive monster boards. The skis were too long for herringbone climbing and mighty heavy for sidestepping. Their users often laced

A mail carrier making his rounds between Colorado towns in the nineteenth century.

strips of animal hides, hair facing backward, to the bottoms of the slats. Another technique was to dip the ski bottoms in water, let it freeze, climb uphill, and then scrape off the ice at the summit of the climb. While the web snowshoes, used by Indians, would have made uphill travel easier, there is no indication that they were used by Colorado settlers until much later.

The most celebrated pioneer of Colorado skiing was John Dyer. "Father" Dyer was a Methodist minister who established churches in Fairplay, Alma, and Breckenridge in the early 1860s. With his poverty-ridden calling, he found it necessary in 1864 to get a mail contract for a route crossing awesome Mosquito Pass to Oro City in California Gulch, where Leadville would later boom. The winter

Mail carrier at the Humbolt Mine near Ouray, 1912.

Lady skiers at Breckenridge, 1889.

Skiers of the Mount Sneffels Snowshoe Club, Ouray, about 1887. They may have invented apres-skiing customs in Colorado.

George R. Porter photo.

snows along the pass had already chopped the life out of his predecessor, Postman John Armstrong.

Dyer carved a pair of skis and had a miserable time learning to use them. He fell constantly while avoiding trees, crossed the clumsy boards on fast downhill runs, and was severely whipped several times by his own pole. At last he mastered the art! The route carried him out after services on Sunday at Fairplay, to Alma and Buckskin Joe for services and mail delivery, over Mosquito Pass to Oro, and then down the Arkansas Canyon to Granite, returning over Weston Pass to South Park in time to reach Fairplay for another Sunday service.

Dyer wasn't the only skiing parson in Colorado's youth. At Lake City, George M. Darley, who built the first church on Colorado's Western Slope, skied the Holy Word, Presbyterian-style, to various mining camps. In the Telluride and Ouray districts, Father James Gibbons held mass for miners in several towns, all threatened by snowslides which often tore down the towering canyon walls. Two miners with whom he had pleaded to stop using the name of the Lord in vain were caught in a massive slide. One escaped, but the other was overwhelmed by the avalanche, which in the priest's words, "ground to mincemeat that tongue which had so often defied the God who made him. It was an appropriate punishment and a warning against sins of the tongue."

One of Colorado's earliest ski races at Irwin, near Crested Butte, 1883. Racing here are Joseph H. Block and Beecher Baney.

Most mountaineers sought mail more than sermons, and most of the carriers skied their winter rounds. Swan Nilson, who carried the pouch from Silverton to Ophir, was apparently buried in a slide December 23, 1883. Efforts to find his body that winter were futile, and later, when someone thought he'd seen Swan whooping it up at a Leadville bar, Silverton residents suspected he had absconded with the Christmas presents he'd been carrying. Great feelings of guilt permeated the community two years later, however, when his remains were found, along with his mailbag and the rotting presents. Postal officials in Denver kept Nilson's decomposed bag on display for years to remind carriers of the dangers faced by their predecessors.

Albert Johnson, a luckless prospector from Canada, took a contract to trek the fearsome route from Crystal over Schofield Pass to Gothic and Crested Butte. Postmen made their tracks on routes from Steamboat to Georgetown, all through the San Juans, and over the high passes of the Sawatch Range.

Babies choose any season in which to be born, and that event often called a Mrs. Suttle, "Master Midwife" at Steamboat Springs, to help deliver them in the "three-wire winters" there, so named for the snow depth on the fences. She was pulled in a toboggan by skiers as far as twenty miles to carry out her duties. Charles Fox Gardiner, a Western Slope doctor, claimed, perhaps tongue in cheek, that once when he became a bit ill on a mercy run, the physician persuaded his mammoth dog, "Czar," to pull him along over a tough trail on skis.

Keeping the mines open all winter long was a demanding challenge for the early ore diggers. James K. Hastings wrote that in the winter of 1871–1872, several of the men at the Montezuma Camp skied down to Denver and back from that isolated spot west of Loveland Pass, a round trip of 110 miles. In Irwin, near Kebler Pass above Crested Butte, Harry C. Cornwall noted in his diary that, during the winter of 1879–1880, the whole town was isolated and miners had to ski over Ohio Pass to get supplies from a ranch north of Gunnison.

Enos Mills, whose nature studies led to the establishment of Rocky Mountain National Park, was only one of several scientists who used skis to make careful observations of the mysteries of mountain winters. They lugged heavy equipment up the mountainsides to record snow depth, measure wind speed, track wildlife patterns, and calculate avalanche probabilities.

Not many old Western movies portrayed cowboys on skis, but many a range rider toted his pair in the winter, briefly abandoning his steed when searching for lost calves in heavy snow-filled woods. Alice Denison of Steamboat Springs wrote in a letter that her cowboy brother bought his skis for $2.50 in 1886. When he undertook to teach

Mr. and Mrs. V. E. Metzler on a ski outing at Crested Butte in the late nineteenth century.

her the skill, she remarked, "It takes the gizzum out of me!" After a few more tries, however, she was able to stand upright all the way down the hill.

Travelers caught in sudden blizzards had to improvise quickly. Aspen's W. B. Devereaux, who wanted to get home for Christmas, was dismayed when the stage he was on had to abandon attempts to cross Independence Pass. He fashioned skis from barrel staves and made it home for the holidays, but spent it in bed from "temporary physical collapse." When the Aspen men decided to throw a Christmas party for the few women in camp, two skiers trekked over Independence Pass to Leadville, fifty miles distant, to obtain oysters with which to stuff the entre.

Trying to pin down when competitive skiing started in Colorado is well-nigh impossible. Swedish immigrants brought the first skis to Aspen and took to racing each other, staking high bets on the outcome. As for written documentation, the sport can be dated from 1883 at Irwin. Early accounts there claim that miners at the Star Mine formed a racing club. Crested Butte had a ski club in 1886, and it competed against a Gunnison club. *Outing* magazine reported several meets that year under the sponsorship of the Gunnison County Snowshoe Club. One of the most spectacular of its races must have been down the face of Tenderfoot Mountain (now "W Mountain") overlooking Gunnison. The slope there is so steep that it would give pause to today's most daring skiers. Pictures from that time also show a Mount Sneffels Snowshoe Club at Ouray, which combined the fun with wining and dining.

The tenderfoot in the mining camps had to learn to ski or endure the scorn of "old-timers" of a winter or more. At White Pine, in the western shadow of Monarch Pass, A. F. Nathan had been taking a ribbing from the grizzled older miners, so he practiced secretly at night. When the crew went up to check diggings on Clover Mountain, Nathan stumbled along in his novice manner, but he showed some savvy in adjusting his skis for the return downhill. His friends urged him on

George Wright goes skiing in fine apparel near Ouray, at the foot of Mount Sneffels. George R. Porter (winter scenes a specialty) photographed this scene about 1888.

with a challenge race for "oysters and cigars," giving him a head start. That night two embarrassed vets reckoned they'd been tricked, never even coming close to Nathan's bombing run down Clover Mountain.

Sooner or later, such antics had to lead to jumping, but the lack of tight bindings made it a dangerous game. Andy Bray used to wait for the Denver and Rio Grande train to enter a deep cut en route from Gunnison to Crested Butte. Then he'd take off down the slope and jump over the engine to the admiration of his viewers and the consternation of the train crew.

Snowslides were the greatest hazard to travel in the mountains, and missing skiers were usually presumed lost from this cause when they were overdue. During an infamous blizzard of 1899, skiers rescued the crew of a train buried near Climax. That same winter, up on Independence Pass (then called Hunter's Pass), a mining camp was marooned, and someone put a sign on the boarding house: "Wanted: 1,000 pairs of Norwegian Snowshoes."

Telephone linemen also used skis, and stories abound about the skill developed by those dutiful innovators, stringing their lines higher as the winter snows increased in depth. Postman Otto McDonald, skiing the Crested Butte mail run, found the snow deep enough to rest himself by leaning on the cross bars of newly-strung telephone poles when he needed a breather.

Early ventures into sport skiing were mostly incidental. The main purpose of skis was to enable people to survive and thrive despite nature's vagaries. While they occasionally raced or jumped, it would remain for Carl Howelsen and several other fun-jumpers to slide through the starting gate to Colorado sport skiing.

Woman ski jumper, Steamboat Springs, about 1918.

Early photo from Howelsen Hill jump, Steamboat Springs.

Chapter Two
The Flying Norseman

After a rousing circus band introduction, "the Big Top" of P. T. Barnum's circus grew silent. Carl Howelsen stood poised on a high platform atop a great chute. Attached to his feet were skis waxed with soap. Then, with a great lunge, he thundered down the chute, sailed off the upturned end over the backs of two elephants and landed on a down slope ramp at the far end of the tent. The crowd went wild and thundered an ovation!

Born in 1877, Howelsen was an immigrant from Norway, where he had already accumulated accolades as a skier, having won the Crown Prince and King's Cups in the famous Holmenkollen meets near Oslo. In 1905, this king of the snowfields journeyed to Germany to repeat his championships at Hamburg. Then he decided to seek adventure in the United States.

In Chicago, Howelsen secured a job as a stonemason, his regular trade, and spent free time at the lakefront amusement park. He was intrigued by a water chute from which people took a thrilling boat ride where the boat shot from the watercourse and onto the lake. To Howelsen, the chute looked a lot like a ski jump, and he soon persuaded the owner to let him try it with soaped skis. Thousands marveled as the wiry, five-foot, seven-inch daredevil sailed out into the lake – among them the manager of Barnum's circus, who immediately signed him up as "the Flying Norseman." For a season, Carl traveled with the circus, but then a fall from the ladder leading to the launch platform prompted him to return to a safer occupation.

Skijoring behind a pung, 1925.

Colorado Ski Museum/Hall of Fame photo.

Hearkening to the lure of the West, Howelsen resumed his career laying stones in Denver. He enjoyed the foothills around the city and built rudimentary ski jumps on winter weekends. By 1911, he and his friend, Agnell Schmidt, started journeying to Hot Sulphur Springs to jump in its deeper powder snow. They soon had such citizens as Horace Button join in the fun. By February of 1912, Hot Sulphur Springs, under Button's enthusiastic leadership, staged the first winter carnival west of the Mississippi River, including the first ski jumping contests.

It was there that Marjorie Perry spotted Howelsen. Marjorie was already a local legend in her hometown of Steamboat Springs. She convinced Carl that Steamboat needed a stonemason and introduced him to the Yampa Valley, cradled by spectacular peaks. After one look,

Three pioneer Steamboat Springs fanatics: Gretta Wither, Donald "Pete" Wither and Dorothy Wither.

Howelsen knew he was in skiers' heaven and took a home in nearby Strawberry Park.

There wasn't much work for a mason in winter at Steamboat, where the snows pile up shoulder-high. Naturally, Howelsen was soon jumping and evoking curious gasps, leaping off mounds in his Norwegian snowshoes. A natural teacher, he soon shared his skill with avid children, setting a precedent which would make Steamboat Springs the foremost producer of ski champions in Colorado. By 1914, Howelsen planned the first winter carnival held in Steamboat, a tradition which has become the longest continuous such event in the state.

For that first carnival, Howelsen designed a ski jump on Woodchuck Hill, overlooking the chugging springs which gave the town its name. A

"Skeeing" at Steamboat Springs, about 1916.

local newspaper was awed by Winter Sport on the Treacherous and Speedy Skee, and celebrated the daring of this hearty newcomer. The carnival also featured women's ski races down the main street, men's cross-country challenges, and children's contests. There were tugs-of-war on skis, wheelbarrow races, and a crawfish race, which required the participants' ankles to be crossed as they skied the course. Skiers had to saw and roll logs, and Boy Scouts had races to build fires and return to the starting line on skis. In later years, skijoring – pulling skiers

behind fast horses—set a tradition of combining the cowboy customs with the winter resort fun in this town of dual infatuations.

Howelsen the spunky stonemason won the jumping competition that first year, soaring 115 feet. The next year a new jump was built just across the river on the steep hill that would later be named Howelsen Hill, site of numerous international records. Ragner Omtvedt took world honors there in 1915 (195 feet) and Henry Hall in 1917 (203 feet).

Jumping team at Dillon in early twenties. Front row: Eyvin Flood, Peter Prestrud. Back row: Hans Hansen, Carl Howelsen, Anders Haugen, Lars Haugen.

Other famous names who showed up to compete at Steamboat were: Peter Prestrud of Dillon, for whom the Dillon jump was later named; James Presteus and Frank Finnegan of Wisconsin; Gunnar Dahle of Parshall, Colorado; and the famed Anders and Lars Haugen, originally from South Dakota. Lars set a new international record in 1919, and Anders garnered an Olympic medal for the United States in 1924. Local skiers also took part in the fun, including Hollis and Marcellus Merrill. Marcellus became the premier inventor of the Colorado ski industry and founded a championship award for the Steamboat Winter Carnival.

Steamboat was not alone. Other areas were infected with ski racing and jumping fever as well. Leadville, Dillon, Frisco, and Denver formed ski

Carl Howelsen's record jump of 192 feet, Steamboat Springs, 1921.

clubs in the 1910s. Eyvin Flood, a Norwegian mining engineer, become famed for his speed skiing in the mining camps of Montezuma and Saint Johns, above Dillon. It was on the Prestrud jump at Dillon that Anders Haugen made a world record 213 foot leap in 1919, and stretched it another foot the next year. In 1921, Howelsen won the national title at Genesee Mountain west of Denver, where the Colorado Mountain Club had built a skiing center.

Despite his love for Steamboat Springs, Howelsen felt it important to return to Oslo in 1922 for his parents' Golden Wedding Anniversary. There, at the age of forty-five, he fell in love with Anna Skarstroen and married her, never making it back to the United States. One child, Leif, was born of that marriage. Leif became a hero of the underground

Horace Button, Hot Sulphur Springs, on the right.

movement in World War II and later wrote his father's biography. Carl continued his skiing career and made his last jump at the age of seventy-one. He died in 1955 and is buried in Oslo. Celebrated as founder of sport skiing in both the Colorado and National Ski Halls of Fame, his greatest living memorial is the tradition for teaching youth to ski in Colorado.

The Steamboat Springs Winter Sport Club, and especially the enthusiasm and efficiency of the Ladies' Recreational Club there, kept skiing very much alive with winter outings and races. Steamboat cheered when local boy James Louis Dalpes made the All-American

Ski Team in 1931. That was also the year when Graeme McGowan, founder of Denver's Arlberg Club, came to town to demonstrate downhill and slalom racing. Shortly after that, United States Olympian John Steele, another Steamboat product, gave a talk for local schools and transported a student named Gordy Wren into ecstasy. Wren, then and there, saw skiing as his career. He is considered by many to be Colorado's greatest all-time, all-around skier. By 1943, Steamboat Springs became the first town in the state to have a public school ski program. It benefited from the coaching of Al Wegeman who had previously taught Denver Boy Scouts to ski the slopes at Genesee Basin.

Those formative years, highlighted by commitment in Steamboat Springs to winter sports, were only one aspect of the gradual frenzy of excitement on Colorado slopes. Down in Denver, the Colorado Mountain Club was getting excited about skiing.

"Old Men's Race" at Hot Sulphur Springs Winter Carnival, 1925.
Colorado Ski Museum/Hall of Fame photo.

29

Genesee Mountain ski jump, 1920s.

Colorado Ski Museum/Hall of Fame photo.

CHAPTER THREE

ARLBERGS, ZIPFELBERGERS AND ESKIMOS

Travelers driving west out of Denver on Interstate 70 cross Genesee Mountain at a point very near the old ski jump built there in 1919 by members of the Colorado Mountain Club. That winter thousands of Denverites flocked up to Genesee to watch flying skiers sail off the strange chute. It was a launching pad for Denver's future as a winter sport center!

Dr. Menefree Howard, head of the Denver Winter Sports Club, bought ten acres there with a lease on 300 more. The site had a thousand-foot run down a hill with a thirty-five percent grade. The first meet featured the Haugen brothers, along with other top nationwide talent. Denver ace Barney Reilly represented the home team, and the open meet even featured seven-year-old Norman Ralston, baptizing junior competition in the state as he took on the masters. By the next year, Genesee hosted the national professional ski meet, with Carl Howelsen taking the crown.

The Colorado Mountain Club was the parent of this group. Formed in 1912, it took winter outings on skis by 1915, having annual outings at Fern and Odessa Lakes in Rocky Mountain National Park. Companion clubs in Colorado Springs, Boulder, and Estes Park formed by the 1920s.

A Lieutenant D'Albizi of the Italian army taught the Denver group to ski on the north slope of the old John Evans estate south of the Denver Country Club. Another popular run was Rilliet Hill, on the sunset slope of Lookout Mountain. Albert Bancroft, reminiscing about those early days, recalled that it was an "open question" whether he'd be allowed on the tramway car with a pair of skis on his way to the foothills.

Ski hut built at Genesee Mountain by Denver clubs.

Several individual ski clubs were spawned by the parent Colorado Mountain Club organization. These included the Rilliet Hill Club, with Lucretia Vaille as its coordinator. Members Neil Grant, Amos Sudler, and Jack Kendrick, gave lessons there and at Homewood Park in Deer Creek Canyon nearby helped by that indomitable lady of the laths, Steamboat's Marjorie Perry. Boulder club members drew the attention of Fox movie producers in 1921, who came to Colorado to film the antics of skiers.

By 1927, the Denver and Rio Grande Railroad was running trains through the new Moffat Tunnel. The west portal, overlooking Middle Park, enticed skiers such as Graeme McGowan, founder of the Arlberg Club in Denver, to remodel tunnel construction cabins into housing for members. That club pioneered the original ski runs which would become

Winter Park. Perennial champion of the Arlberg races was Frank Ashley, who dominated the Colorado race scene until Gordon Wren and Barney McLean came along. The Berthoud Pass route to Winter Park was closed in winters until 1933, so Denverites paid $2.25 for the round trip fare on the train from Union Station.

Other popular Denver ski outings in those spirited days included Brook Forest, Chicago Lake, Homewood Park, Nederland and Lake Eldora, Lost Park, and St. Mary's Glacier. Colorado Springs' Pikes Peak Club sojourned at Green Mountain Falls and Bald Mountain.

Both ski techniques and ski bindings were improving. Norway's Sondried Norheim revolutionized jumping when he invented a woven willow binding, permitting use of shorter skis. By 1931, cable bindings had been invented in Switzerland. Three years later, steel edging was

Sparse snowflakes had to be gathered in foothills for spring skiing at Genesee Mountain, 1920s.

The cross pole had shrunk before use of two poles became popular. No special bindings were required in the early days at Genesee Mountain.

added to skis. By the mid-thirties, Thor Groswold started Denver's own ski factory at Twelfth and Shoshone streets and produced some of the nation's best hickory slats.

International interest in the West Portal–Berthoud Pass region started in 1936, with famed Dartmouth coach Otto Schneibs and European champion Florian Haemerle both teaching there. Regular ski buses supplemented the trains.

Denver skiers in the early thirties.

Colorado Ski Museum/Hall of Fame photo.

Down in Denver, Dick Thompkins suggested a Colorado Winter Sports Council, forerunner of the Rocky Mountain Ski Association. The Council was chartered in 1936, with both Nordic and Alpine divisions. Nordic included jumping and cross–country racing. Alpine included downhill and the slaloms. A four-way meet included all of these, but very few skiers ever entered all contests. (Colorado's only skier ever to qualify in all four events in the Olympics was Gordy Wren in 1948.)

In 1937, the May Company, a Denver department store, put up financing for the first rope tow in Colorado at Berthoud Pass. It started operation on February 7, 1937. A tragedy occurred close to the area that day when two refugees from Hitler's Germany were caught in a snowslide. Probing by inexperienced members of a nearby Civilian

Denver skiers, around 1938.

Colorado Ski Museum/Hall of Fame photo.

Conservation Corps camp had no results, but with the spring melt-off the bodies were found, one mutilated with a pole hole through it.

Denver ski enthusiasts often met for lunch at the Navarre Restaurant downtown, led by such enthusiasts as Myron Neusteter, Charles Boettcher, and Jack Kendrick. Out of one such meeting came the idea of chartering a ski trip to Sun Valley. The group arrived there on Washington's Birthday, 1937, and were hosted personally by Averell Harriman, who served hot mulled wine at the warming house on Dollar Mountain, as all delighted to the music of Eddie Duchin's popular dance band. The ski mystique caught the Denverites, and they dreamed of their own ski lodge. Frank Bulkley and J. C. Blickensderfer decided that the village of Empire would be ideal, and many pitched in for the financing. Bob Balch said the new building looked like a trap door spider's nest, so it gained the moniker, The Trap Door.

Ski jumper at Genesee Mountain, 1920s.

McClure photo.

Ski course and picnic at Genesee Mountain.

Thor Groswold and Dick Thompkins sparked a new racing club, Zipfelberger, while Frank Bulkey, who sold ski equipment, founded the Eskimo Ski Club. Then, Fred Bellmar organized the Colorado Ski Runners to lure Denver's younger generation out to the slopes. By 1938, Thompkins opened a regular ski shop at 1360 Broadway, now the site of the Colorado Heritage Center. Until that time, gear had to be purchased at the old Tritch Hardware Company. The Ski Shop and its later branch operation in the May Company continued until World War II travel restrictions depleted the market.

The Zipfelbergers chose the eastern slope of Loveland Pass, just below timberline, for their lodge. A favorite run, though, was Porcupine

Skiers getting off the train at West Portal, late 1930s.

Gulch, far down the western slope. It was there that Groswold and Blickensderfer set up a portable ski tow in 1938. It was a four and one-half horsepower engine mounted on a toboggan with a thousand feet of rope strung by pulleys and fastened to trees or snow anchors. The whole rig, which they called the "Little Sweden Freezer Company," could be transported in a station wagon. Another group of skiers built a lodge a mile above the Jones Pass turnoff on Berthoud Pass, calling it Red Mountain Lodge.

Colorado's first fatality from sport skiing, other than by avalanche, occurred when Berrien Hughes ran into a rock on Loveland Pass on May 21, 1939. Hughes Run at Winter Park was later named in his memory.

Denver skiers aboard the skier special train through Moffat Tunnel in the late 1930s.

By the winter of 1938–1939, the informal ski patrol at Berthoud Pass recorded 50,000 skier–days, an increase of 20,000 from the year before. This increase in activity prompted the Colorado Mountain Club to form the Southern Rocky Mountain Ski Association for clubs in Wyoming, New Mexico, and Colorado. Frank Ashley was its first president. Evelyn Runnette was appointed secretary and supervised the hub of its operations for many dedicated years to come.

By that time, Coloradoans were flushed by the success of the "dark horse" team which had captured the Jeffers Cup at Sun Valley the winter before. Friedl Pfeifer, instructor at Sun Valley, gave them their initial lessons in slalom after they arrived, and the victors startled the veterans. After the Colorado team came home to a hero's welcome, they

A Grand Lake school teacher takes a ski lesson from Johnny Johnson back in the early twenties.

Skiing at Winter Park in March 1940.

---

sponsored their own meet at Berthoud. The next year, Colorado's first Kandahar Race was held. It was the worldwide daddy of all slaloms, named for the town in Afghanistan where a British victory had occurred, and first held in Switzerland in 1911.

"Denver's New Winter Playground" was the headline in 1938 for plans by Denver Parks and Improvements Manager George Cranmer's plan to develop the Winter Park ski area as a part of the Denver Mountain Parks system. City workers volunteered their weekends clearing the slopes, and Cranmer combined Federal Public Works Administration funds, Denver city funds and popular donations to provide $50,000 for the project. Bob Balch laid out the trails, Jack Kendrick led the fund

Proper attire for all ages, about 1921.

drives, and the Civilian Conservation Corps and United States Forest Service provided labor. A Comstam T-bar lift was installed to make riding up a simple matter compared to the awkward rope tows. By 1941, the whole operation was going strong. By that time, however, two other areas in the state already had chairlifts – Pioneer on Cement Creek north of Gunnison and Red Mountain at Glenwood Springs.

A race meet at West Portal-Winter Park area, before World War II.

Some purists complained that all this business of ski tows ruined "true skiing."

Considering all this furious effort by the Mile High City, one might get the impression that sport skiing grew out of Denver and was introduced to the hinterland mountaineers. Not so! Dozens of mountain towns formed clubs, built tows, groomed slopes, and took a new look at the winters, previously considered paralyzing, with cheerful anticipation.

Early San Juan "snoeshoers"

P. David Smith photo.

Chapter Four

Way Up Yonder in the Mountains

During the turbulent twenties and the lean thirties, there was hardly any slope near a Colorado mountain town that wasn't pocked with the sitzmarks of local skiers. One could start anywhere in the high altitudes to recount the antics of local fanatics who carved the winter snows and spent their summers clearing the runs.

Because it was a small town full of college students who tended toward boredom in winter's isolation, Gunnison may have been a shade more intense during those years with its outings on the slats. Cut off in all directions by mountain passes which often closed following the winter solstice, the town had to fend off cabin fever. In 1916, Moses Amos Jencks, a business professor at Western State College, started skiing as a regular sport, with token credit given for the training. Joined by local enthusiasts, students made short runs around the town, but for deeper drifts, they took the narrow-gauge train to Quick's Hill near Crested Butte, twenty-eight miles to the north.

Embers of the old Gunnison Ski Club were fanned to life again in 1938, when three Gunnison men, Wes McDermott, Rial Lake, and Charles Schweitzer, planned a special excursion train to Marshall Pass between Gunnison and Salida. The train itself served as a ski lift as the crowd zoomed down to the water tank at Shawano, 700 feet below the summit, and then were hauled back to the top for another run. Expert ski-maker Thor Groswold, Aspen's T. J. Flynn, and Count Phillipe de Pret, Broadmoor Hotel instructor, joined to teach finer points.

Western State College and Gunnison skiers John Knowles, Rial Lake, and Jack Gorsuch, in the 1930s.

While cold, Gunnison doesn't get nearly the snow of the Crested Butte area; so the club chose Cement Creek, about twenty miles north, as the site for the Pioneer ski area. In 1939, using abandoned tram cables and towers from the Blistered Horn mine above the mining camp of Tin Cup, workers hand-crafted chairs to make the first chairlift in Colorado. To the dismay of those weekend engineers, the lift had to be rebuilt several times because of varying snow depths. Its Big Dipper run was dangerous, and the Forest Service condemned the run several times, but Pioneer continued operation until 1951, when the club and college shifted over to Rozman Hill, a safer slope near Crested Butte.

Ski tourers were venturing out, crossing the overwhelming peaks that lie between Aspen and Crested Butte. In his book, American Skiing, Otto Schneibs wrote of an expedition out of Ashcroft, ten miles south of Aspen, which included champion skiers Steve Bradley, Dick Durrance, and George Cranmer. The group crossed formidable Pearl

St. Mary's Glacier had year-round skiing with a special ski meet on the Forth of July.

Pass and skied down into Crested Butte. Today, adventurous skiers trek over a half dozen passes in that region, with the Western State Ski Team making its annual preseason conditioning run through the rugged Elk Mountains there.

Ashcroft, a mining ghost town, was chosen in 1936 to become Colorado's premier ski resort. Tom Flynn, a pioneer of Aspen's Roaring Fork valley, met Billy Fiske, an international sportsman who had won the 1932 Olympic bobsled races in California. After visiting several of the big resorts there, the pair decided to build their own Highland Bavarian Lodge at Ashcroft. Flynn had heard about the commercial prospect of skiing at Aspen, first suggested as early as 1922. Aspenites, however, were awaiting another silver boom, looking wistfully at the old mine dumps playing leapfrog down the face of Smuggler Mountain.

Skiers of the Mount Sneffels Snowshoe Club, Ouray, about 1887. They may have invented apres-skiing customs in Colorado.

George R. Porter photo.

Ashcroft, at the foot of mighty Hayden Peak, interested investors Robert Rowen and Ted Ryan. Flynn enticed Swiss ski expert Andre Roch to survey proposed trails, with a vision of an aerial tramway which would cost millions. With Aspen city lots going for $5.00 each in those days, financing was a problem which even the State of Colorado tried to solve with the issuance of bonds to underwrite the venture. Funding crept in so slowly that when Europe went to war in 1939, the plan was still a dream. Fiske enlisted in the Royal Air Force in England and became the first American pilot to lose his life in the conflict. Flynn, disheartened, suspended the Ashcroft dream.

Aspen had, however, sipped of the commercial ski brew and become intoxicated. Roch had taken one look at mighty Ajax Mountain, which towered 3,000 feet over Monarch Street on the east side of town. He declared it a great ski site, and in 1937, the Roaring Fork Ski Club

Aspen's old boat tow.

Paul Hauk photo.

---

began building trails. The club went on to construct a boat tow, one of three in the state. (The other two were at Steamboat Springs and Homewood, southwest of Denver.) The boat tow was a cumbersome pair of eight passenger sleds counter-balanced on an old mine hoist. One hazard at Aspen was a gully to be crossed on a snow bridge. When the boat veered off course, it dropped its passengers twenty feet into the ravine.

Among the visitors who came to admire the Aspen development was Elizabeth Paepcke, wife of Walter Paepcke, founder of the Container Corporation of America. She would one day show Aspen to her husband who would touch off big-time skiing in Colorado.

In 1939, Aspen was host to the Southern Rocky Mountain Alpine races, and by 1941, Roch Run was the site of the National Alpines. That event brought champions Toni Matt and Dick Durrance, who had

Telluride Ski Club. 1924

Billy Mahoney, Sr. photo.

an instant love affair with Ajax. Others who took part were Bill Janss, Barney McLean, Alf Engen, Gordy Wren, and Darcy Brown. Brown, whose name was David Robinson Crocker Brown, Jr., simplified that to D.R.C. Brown, but people usually called him Darcy. He had inherited much of the Aspen land, and his name would be interwoven with the epic of Aspen's greatest days.

Other areas weren't letting the snow melt under their feet, either. In Summit County people flocked to Hoosier Pass above Breckenridge. St. Mary's Glacier was famed for its Fourth of July ski events. People in the southern part of the state skied at Wolf Creek Pass, developed by Kelly Boyce and friends. The snow level there is the greatest in the state – 500 to 600 inches a year! Federal Depression funds and Mayor Mike Ferno of Salida opened Monarch Pass, with the lodge being called Inn Ferno.

Summer skiing in the Great Sand Dunes, 1930s. Pictured are Jerry Hart, Karl Arndt and Carl Blaurock.

Colorado Ski Museum/Hall of Fame photo.

At Glenwood Springs, J. E. Sayer donated land on Red Mountain to the city, and the winter sports club worked with the visionary Wilfred "Slim" Davis of the Forest Service to build a chairlift, which opened in January of 1942. Alas, it was just in time for World War II travel restrictions to dampen the enterprise.

Other ski areas operating well before World War II were at Estes Park, Allenspark, Grand Lake, Creede, Cumbres Pass, Hot Sulphur Springs, and Glen Cove. At Glen Cove, the Pikes Peak Ski Club had a rope tow first run by a Model A Ford, but then the club graduated to a Buick. Estes Park hosted the 1934 Nationals, with local skier J.J. Duncan, Jr. winning the downhill, and Steamboat's D. Monson grabbing the Nordic title.

Hot Sulphur Springs never forgot its leadership. It gave starts to Horace Button, James L. Harsh, and Robert "Barney" McLean, all of

Early day skiers on Telluride mountain.

whom became outstanding champions. It broadened out into what the local newspaper called "skisport," with skating, hockey, and tobogganing.

Louise A. White of Fort Collins was Colorado's pioneer in women's ski competitions. Starting on the slopes at Idledale in 1931, she competed at Berthoud, Genesee, and Glen Cove, and in 1937 won first place in the ladies' division of downhill, slalom, and combined at the United States Amateur Ski Association Championships at Berthoud. Continuing to garner national ribbons, she founded the Colorado Skiing Association exclusively for women of the snow.

On the western edge of Colorado, skiing thrived on Grand Mesa, one of the largest flat-topped mountains in the world. Cedaredge, clinging under the rim of the mesa, boasted the longest skiing season in the state except for St. Mary's Glacier. Delta and Grand Junction skiers weekended at Land's End on the mesa, a sheer drop into the Gunnison valley below, and tested the north rim, which would eventually emerge as Powderhorn. Durango skiers favored Chapman Hill, near the modern Tamarron resort, or ventured to Silverton or Telluride.

Two miles above sea level, the highest incorporated city in North America was Leadville. It was a natural site for skiing, but most of the activities centered on even higher Climax, site of the Climax Molybdenum Mine on Fremont Pass. It would become the largest underground mine in North America, and in 1936, the firm developed a ski area that featured lighted slopes for night skiing, thus joining Steamboat Springs which had already lit up Howelsen Hill with automobile lights.

It was up in Leadville country that the most significant contribution to modern skiing would take place. The United States Army chose a valley near Leadville as a site for the training of its mountain troops, gathering the cream of the nation's ski experts to Colorado, along with a number of novices. They discovered a ski wonderland at Camp Hale and returned to build a ski empire.

Pioneer Ski Area and its infamous Big Dipper Run, 1939.
Genevive Hice photo.

1936/37 Bob Mahoney skiing on Kids Hill, Telluride.

Bill Mahoney Sr. photo.

CHAPTER FIVE

CAMP HALE, THE BIG CHRISTY OF COLORADO SKIING

Camp Hale grew out of a lettuce patch! The amazing but successful attempts to grow lettuce at the little town of Pando, just over Tennessee Pass from Leadville, were a desperation measure in the thirties. This station on the Denver and Rio Grande Railroad was a stop for icing refrigerator cars. Pando had once been a minor mining camp, nestled in the evening shadows of the mighty Mount of the Holy Cross, but fate had deserted it.

Soldiers stationed there could hardly believe the isolation, calling it the "Shangri-la of the Rockies." At 9,200 feet above sea level, life was hard and many suffered from a cough they called the "Pando Hack," the result of coal stoves in barracks and train smoke that hung in the valley for days on end. On the other hand, scenery and skiing were magnificent, and the camp proved a perfect place for mountaineer preparation of the famous Tenth Mountain Division. The Viking Battalion of the Ninety-ninth Infantry from Camp Ripley, Minnesota, also trained at Camp Hale and later was the first unit to liberate Norway on May 8, 1945.

Early in World War II, Finnish ski troops stalemated the Russian invasion of their land. Minot "Minnie" Dole, founder of the United States National Ski Patrol, along with some other skiing leaders, pondered the Finnish defense system and concluded that the United States did not have any similar program. While several army units had small patrols, the training was spasmodic and the units scattered. In 1940, Dole was able to convince Army Chief of Staff George C. Marshall of the need for such a unit and the Eighty-seventh Mountain Infantry Regiment was formed. Dole used the National Ski

Camp Hale, located on the west side of Tennessee Pass, near Leadville. It was home of the famed Tenth Mountain Division and trained 10,000 men during World War II in ski and mountain warfare.

Association to recruit experienced skiers and mountaineers as an initial cadre.

Initially, training was at Fort Lewis, Washington, while the army considered several sites for the special program. West Yellowstone was discounted because it was the breeding ground for the almost extinct trumpeter swan. After Billy Fiske was shot down in European combat, his partner, Ted Ryan, offered the Ashcroft site to the army, but it was too far from a good railhead. Pando was finally chosen because it had good rail and highway facilities and was well isolated, yet close to a town with housing for construction laborers. The camp was named after Brigadier General Irving Hale, a West Pointer from Denver.

Dole's recruiting drive took off in a big way, with some of the nation's top experts signing on, along with a myriad of novices. Many foreign skiers

Soldiers of the Tenth Mountain Division at Camp Hale in 1943.

also enrolled, and about five hundred of them received their naturalization papers at Leadville. The great Hannes Schneider, Friedl Pfeifer, Gordy Wren, Bob Balch, Larry Jump, Harald "Pop" Sorensen, Walter Praeger, Torger Tokle, John Jay, Steve Knowlton, Robert W. Parker, Peter Seibert, Rudy Schnackenberg, and Toni Matt, all joined the Hale operation. Even George Frankenstein, son of the former German Ambassador to England, signed up.

Leadville had a reputation as one of the wildest of "Wild West" towns, and the army placed it off limits for their innocent soldiers. Local leaders were outraged by the ban and went to work to close down the red light district (officially, at least) and set up services for venereal disease control. Their purification rites went so far as to pass sanitation laws for the entire city, although some citizens, treasuring their traditional independence,

Camp Hale soldiers training at Resolution Creek, overlooking Camp Hale, during World War II.
Colorado Ski Museum/Hall of Fame photo.

thought the laws went a bit too far. At last, by February of 1942, the army lifted its "Off Limits" sign and Camp Hale troops could travel into Leadville for R & R.

That brief ban may have cost Leadville the position that Aspen would eventually fill in post-war skiing, as soldiers frustrated at their isolation, took the train to Aspen, where they found slopes with snow as good as that at Leadville. Aspen was also on the maneuver circuit of Camp Hale. Leadville was booming again, with military construction crews building facilities for 15,000 men, and mines reopened to produce strategic war minerals. An active mining camp lacks the charm and quietude some romantically believe should pervade ski resorts. Then there was the decisive factor. Mrs. Walter Paepcke had fallen in love with Aspen, not Leadville.

Camp Hale left some buildings as service structures for Cooper Hill after World War II.

Numerous stories abound regarding Camp Hale's war games. Some people maintained that artillery blasts caused the rockfall which filled in one arm of the cross that made the Mount of the Holy Cross a national monument and venerated shrine, but the small artillery pieces used never shoot that far. Another tale relates a mock war in the Aspen area in which a unit became hopelessly lost on Red Mountain. The commander of the unit gave up looking for his men and checked into Aspen's Hotel Jerome for a good rest while his charges wandered into town in disarray, angry and frostbitten.

Temperatures at Camp Hale dipped as low as minus 40°F., and ordinary rules of camping had to be drastically revised. More appropriate equipment was devised. For instance, the metal zippers on clothing and bags stuck, tearing flesh from anguished fingers. Tents collapsed in deep snowfalls,

Infantry training at Camp Hale, on the Continental Divide near Leadville.

and Arctic explorer Dr. Vilhjamer Stefansson was brought in to teach troops how to construct snow houses. Forerunners of modern snowmobiles and snowcats also had their trial days there.

The Eighty-seventh Regiment grew into the Tenth Mountain Division, a unit that would win the highest accolades for skill and bravery in combat. Colonel Onslow S. Rolfe, nicknamed "Pinkie," was commander. A great mountaineering man, he learned his skiing at Hale under the tutelage of photographer John Jay. The troops had to take some ribbing from the prestigious *New Yorker* magazine, founded, published, and edited by colorful, Aspen-born Harold Ross, who accused "Minnie's Ski Troops" of having a ski club assignment to sit out the war. Ouch! Camp Hale was one of the toughest training centers in the nation. The only touches of glamour came when actress Jinx Faulkenberg came for a visit or when Warner Brothers Studio filmed a documentary there.

Thor Groswold's Denver factory won a contract to make skis for the Tenth, and those surplus white boards – camouflage skis – along with cumbersome white boots would become a fad among skiers in post-war days – "Camp Hale chic."

Atop Tennessee Pass, the military built its main downhill run, with the longest T-bar in the world at that time. This was Cooper Hill, and after the war it was shared with Lake County and eventually turned over entirely to civilians.

"Pinkie" Rolfe was replaced by Major General George P. Hayes when the unit was combat-ready. Hayes, a World War I Congressional Medal of Honor winner who had seven horses shot out from under him, found the Tenth toughened by winter blasts, tenuous climbs over granite cliffs, and leagues of hard-slogging mule skinning. The "Ski Club Boys" reached Italy in 1944, plunging into some of the deadliest encounters of the war. They took Riva Ridge, Buio, Prada, Mount Belvadere, Mount della Vedetto and, finally, spearheaded the conclusive Po River Valley attack.

The unit was decimated. A total of 992 were killed, including Colorado's famed Bob Balch and Torger Tokle, the champion Norwegian skier who had become a U.S. citizen at the Lake County courthouse in Leadville. Friedl Pfeifer had a lung shot out, and scores of others were injured. No wonder that General Mark Clark called the Tenth the finest division he'd ever seen.

In the summer of 1945, the survivors were sent home and issued their discharges and uniforms with the proud symbol of crossed bayonets. Camp Hale was mostly dismantled–some say by bureaucratic error. Remnants were left standing for a few years and included in Fort Carson (Colorado Springs) field training operations. When the Korean War broke out, Cooper Hill echoed once more with the call of "Track!" as a new generation of soldiers gained their first ski legs and succumbed to the joy of Colorado snow. Later, the camp was used for war games such as Operation Ski Jump in 1954, Hail Storm in 1955,

Close-order drill on skis at Camp Hale during World War II.

and Cold Spot and Lode Star Baker in 1956. Army entries in Olympic and other contests trained there from time to time. Then, on July 4, 1965, the army administered the coup de grace to the Pando encampment, turning it over to the General Services Administration for disposal.

The Rocky Mountain Chapter of the Tenth Mountain Division Veterans erected a monument on Tennessee Pass, explaining the bleak foundations in the valley below and listing the names of those killed in action. With frequent reunions at Vail, just over Shrine Pass, many of the Division members don't have far to travel, because they moved to Colorado after the war, taking up business and professional pursuits, and, of course, getting involved in commercial skiing.

Tenth Mountain veterans were so influential in post–war Colorado ski development that at least a few should be mentioned. Friedl Pfeifer sparked Aspen's development, along with his buddies Johnny Litchfield (who opened the Red Onion saloon there), Len Woods, Dick Wright, and Fritz Benedict. Benedict, a graduate of Frank Lloyd Wright's School of Architecture, designed buildings for the Aspen Humanities Institute, Aspen Highlands, and Snowmass-at-Aspen. Curt Chase ran the Aspen Ski School after Friedl went to develop Buttermilk. Oregon's Toni Matt showed up in Aspen, as did Robert W. Parker and Pete Seibert, who moved on to develop Vail after cultivating the Roaring Fork resort. The Tenth's official photographer, John Jay, furnished the main lens for Aspen and skiing in general.

Gordy Wren taught all over the West, as did Walter Praeger. Leon Wilmot instructed at Ski Broadmoor, where Steve Knowlton managed the operation between founding Aspen's Golden Horn and heading up Colorado Ski Country USA. Bob Sayer was a prime mover of Powderhorn Ski Area. Crosby Perry-Smith and Pop Sorensen instructed at Winter Park, Paul Duke at Breckenridge. Karl Boehm bought and developed the ski touring lodge of Peaceful Valley. Rudy Schnackenberg managed Steamboat's Howelsen Hill, while Barney McLean came home to Hot Sulphur Springs and became a general skiing consultant. Larry Jump developed Arapahoe Basin. Gerry Cunningham founded Gerry's Mountain Sports to supply skiing and mountaineering equipment. Merrill Hastings published *Ski* magazine in Denver. The list could go on, inexorably tying the heritage of Camp Hale to Colorado skiing.

Tourism, one of Colorado's vital industries, had hardly been touched by the national interest in winter sports. That was all about to be changed as these vets, along with other, newer faces, lined up at the top of the hill for a magnificent slalom into prosperity.

T-bar tow at Aspen, 1947.

CHAPTER SIX

PAEPCKE, PFEIFER AND POWDER

Friedl Pfeifer first became enamored with Aspen as a Camp Hale instructor. He met with townspeople there in 1943 to share his hope of coming back after the war to build a ski area far greater than that the little boat tow serviced.

By Memorial Day of 1945, Elizabeth Paepcke had saved enough gasoline rationing coupons to drive with her husband, Walter, from their ranch south of Denver to Aspen. She wanted to show him what had so enchanted her back in 1938, on her first visit. Walter Paepcke took one look around, and in the same decisive and commanding manner by which he had built the Container Corporation of America into a major industrial firm, settled on his own plans for the quiet village.

Add one Pfeifer and one Paepcke to one mountain of powder snow, and a most delightful explosion ensued!

Walter Paepcke was from Chicago, where he had been heir to his father's Chicago Mill and Lumber Company. Born in 1896, he was favored with a classical education at Chicago's Latin School and then Yale, where he studied economics and German literature. He had the rare gift of a combination of business sense and love of culture. In 1922, he married Elizabeth Nitze, daughter of a Romance language professor, William A. Nitze. In 1926, Paepcke established a packaging business to improve cardboard box shipping. His brilliance in design and marketing made it a remarkable success, enabling him to broaden his investments, including the purchase of a Colorado ranch.

Friedl Pfeifer was an Austrian who came to lead the ski school at Sun Valley in 1936. When World War II involved the United States, he

Skiers enjoy Winter Park and their new metal edge skis.

Robert Smilanic photo.

was imprisoned in North Dakota as an enemy alien, but soon the authorities realized their mistake and he joined the American ski troopers as an instructor in the Tenth Mountain Division. Wounded in combat, Friedl was recuperating in a California hospital when Paepcke telephoned him and arranged a meeting to discuss their mutual ambitions.

Paepcke then obtained the services of another talented Austrian refugee, Herbert Bayer, to take charge of planning for the Aspen project. Even as the ink congealed on the Japanese surrender documents, Paepcke was meeting with Aspen citizens and offering free paint to spruce up the appearance of the town. While some were reluctant to follow his lead, others were enthusiastic about the prospects of a new source of income for their struggling community.

Ski racers before a big meet at Aspen in its early days.

The industrialist proposed to build two chairlifts, one of which would be the longest such lift in the world, up Ajax Mountain, later called simply Aspen Mountain. United States Forest Service rangers completed the paperwork involving the White River National Forest in 1946, and Paepcke was able to attract investors. Among those investors were George Berger, Jr. of Denver's Colorado National Bank; Paepcke's brother-in-law, Paul Nitze, who soon became U. S. Secretary of the Navy; and Conrad Hilton, the hotel magnate.

Another prime investor was Darcy Brown, Jr., a hardy pioneer of Denver ski clubs and heir to his father's mining and ranching interests in the Aspen area. A descendent of the town's founders, Brown had maintained the estate through the Depression years and now owned many fine holdings there. Paepcke founded the Aspen Company and

purchased a parcel of land from Brown which included Aspen Meadows, where the Chicagoan would build a humanities institute. The Aspen Company also leased the venerable Hotel Jerome from Lawrence Elisha.

Chairlifts were constructed under the direction of Aspen engineer Harold "Red" Rowland, a vital cog in the ski program. Along with Frank Ashley and Dick Durrance, Rowland would take his turn as mountain manager. When Rowland retired in 1976 as vice president of engineering, he had also directed construction of the lifts at Buttermilk, Snowmass, and Breckenridge. Rowland completed the initial lift by December of 1946, and to try out the new course, Aspenites ran the first Roch Cup Races held in honor of Andre Roch who had first envisioned the future of the mountain. Paepcke donated the prizes, won by Barney McLean and Barbara Kidder.

Before the crowds showed up, a ski patrol was needed. Colorado had been a forerunner in realizing the importance of ski patrols under the leadership of Denver alpine racer Edward F. Taylor, second director of the National Ski Patrol. Aspen created a model crew to control the hill's mobile population.

Friedl Pfeifer skiing Aspen, 1947.

Lloyd Arnold photo.

For Aspen's Grand Opening on January 11, 1947, a special vista-dome train came from Denver, loaded with the governor and other notables. It was met by a torchlight gathering with the United States Army Band and Tenth Mountain Division color guard. Alas, there was not an inch of snow on the streets! Following a parade the next day, Edith Robinson, daughter of the mayor, pushed the button starting the giant lifts moving. The crowd rode up to the Sun Deck, at 11,300 feet, where the snow was deep but the band's tuba player was a bit short of breath. Johnny Litchfield, Master of Ceremonies, presented a plaque from the Aspen

Aspen's Fred Iselin, 1950.

ski troop veterans, after which the skiers took off on the old Roch's Run and a rudimentary Spar Gulch trail.

Famed national champion Dick Durrance moved to Aspen as mountain manager and Fred Iselin deserted Sun Valley to serve as principal instructor. New trails were cut, including Ruthie's Run, named for Darcy Brown's wife. A start on social life was found at Litchfield's Red Onion and Steve Knowlton's Golden Horn, which he built through a labor of love. The Golden Horn was only the first of several Colorado restaurants Knowlton would operate.

Skiing was only one side of Walter Paepcke's grand design for Aspen. His plan to make it an intellectual and cultural mecca involved Chancellor of the University of Chicago, Robert Hutchins, and philosopher Mortimer Adler, as well as other famous thinkers. This intellectual circle around Paepcke moved Aspen into a unique world of mental excitement to match the physical challenges of skiing as the Aspen Institute for Humanistic Studies burst forth!

The summer of 1949 marked the bicentennial of the birth of the German literary giant, Johan Goethe. Paepcke, who prided himself on his ability to memorize passages from Goethe's Faust, saw it as an event to celebrate, and he convinced Albert Schweitzer, one of the world's foremost philosophers, to make his first journey to the United States. Then seventy-four years of age, the Nobel Prize winner became the centerpiece of the event, joined by such famous figures as Ortega y Gasset, Arthur Rubinstein, Pulitzer Prize winner Thornton Wilder, Dorothy Maynor, Erica Morini, Nathan Milstein, and Dmitiri Metropoulos and his Minneapolis Symphony. Aspen soared into the highest levels of intellectual and cultural thought in one leap, as the event drew thousands and worldwide publicity. Adler explained that Aspen was to symbolize the Athenian ideal of arete, a perfect mind in a perfect body, and saw the institute as a new concept of leisure, positively directed, in America.

Skiers gathered in front of Aspen's Jerome Hotel in 1939.

A second shot of world publicity came the following winter when Aspen hosted the Federation Internationale de Ski (FIS) bi-annual world championships, lured by Dick Durrance. This combination of events would make Aspen the best known Colorado community outside of Denver. The FIS brought the world's greatest ski masters to Aspen Mountain, including Stein Eriksen from Norway, Zeno Colo from Italy, and Andrea Mead, who married champion David Lawrence. Sweden commanded cross-country honors; Norway's Hans Bjornstad made the winning glide off Willoughby Jump. Several of the greatest, including Eriksen, Mead, and Lawrence, came to Colorado for good.

Hooked on skiing, Aspen started a junior ski program directed by Steve Knowlton, who trained such youth as Bill Marolt, Myke Baar, Sharon Pejak, Jimmy Heuga, and Dick Durrance, Jr. as well as other future champs. By 1951, the resort held its first Winterskol, its own special brand of winter carnival.

View from the top of Aspen, 1951.

Robert Smilanic photo.

Paepcke lived to see the fruition of his dreams for the old mining town, having sold his shares in the Aspen Skiing Corporation to Paul Nitze. Aspen added an annual design conference, remodeled its Wheeler Opera House into a platform for famous speakers, and hosted musicians who founded the famed Aspen Music Festival. Corporate leaders gathered at the Executive Institute to broaden their humanistic perspective with discussions of Plato and Nietzsche. Paepcke died in 1960, having transformed Aspen and having brought a new image to Colorado.

Meanwhile, W.B.N. "Whip" Jones established a whole new ski area nearby, naming it Aspen Highlands. Friedl Pfeifer set up Buttermilk for beginning and more cautious skiers, broadening the attractions of the resort. Aspen became unique to the American scene and perhaps the world scene. There are many great ski areas, but few with the superb cultural attractions and glamour of this one, which attracted even more

Aspen's original chairlift, a result of the dreams of Paepcke and Pfeifer.

Fred Iselin taking his ease and his lunch while directing activities at Aspen Highlands.
Colorado Ski Museum/Hall of Fame photo.

famous personalities than Sun Valley. Aspen had an intellectual aura of the Ivy League and rang with the sound of music, ranging from quality jazz to classics old and new. It was also the place for any champion skier to perform at least some of his great feats, and many stayed there to live.

While Aspen became Colorado's cosmopolitan island, echoing with many languages, it was not alone in the skiing field. All of Colorado was leaping ahead following World War II, and ski resorts were soon dotting the map in all directions, most of them mildly oblivious to the Aspen phenomenon.

Parking area at Loveland Basin, 1940s.

Loveland Basin's double chairlift, first in the nation, 1947.

CHAPTER SEVEN

PROSPECTING THE POWDER

Larry Jump paused, leaning on his ski poles, and gazed out at the great white bowl on the western rim of Loveland Pass. This was skiing! This was freedom!

Born to a California skiing family, Larry had performed with the Dartmouth College team. Graduating in 1936, he went to work with the International Labor Office in Geneva and volunteered as an ambulance driver for France when the war broke out. He was taken prisoner by the Germans, but they released him to the United States Consulate in 1940, after which he joined the ski troops at Camp Hale and served as a combat intelligence officer. Now, with his white slats checked in, he was employed by the Denver Chamber of Commerce to survey possible ski areas. His partner in this venture was Frederick "Sandy" Schauffler, who had skied for Amherst College before the war.

Arapahoe Basin, Colorado's highest ski area, filled a wide and lonesome cirque along the road west of Loveland Pass. Few people lived up there, except for Max and Edna Dercum and their children, Sunni and Rolf, who had the Ski Tip Ranch near the modern Keystone resort. It was named for broken ski tips, left by guest skiers and used as door latches at the lodge. A Cornell University skier, Max became a forestry professor and ski coach at Penn State and was assigned a research project at Mount Evans. He bought the ranch and moved the family there in 1942, founding their own ski lodge. Dercum met Larry Jump and Sandy Schauffler and helped with their survey. Soon he was involved in building a ski course with them.

The trio joined ski manufacturer Thor Groswold and national champion Dick Durrance to form Arapahoe Basin, Inc. in 1946. A war surplus

Steamboat Springs' winning ski team, March 7, 1948. Left to right: #7 Alvin Scoggans; #13 LaVerne Marshall; #25 Gary Regan; #31 G. Knowles; #1 Marvin Crawford; #43 Buddy Werner; Coach Al Wegeman.

truck hauled skiers from the original lodge to a rope tow midway up the slope. Then Max decided some towers could be constructed from nearby forested mining claims, and the "Thick and Thin Lumber Company" mill was formed. With financing as slow as syrup from an ice jug, they contracted with Colorado's growing Heron Brothers Construction Company to build a lift. Heron became the leading lift builder in the state for many years. By the 1948–1949 season, two chairlifts carried 13,000 skiers up the basins, while the Dercums dreamed of more accommodations as Dillon's Wildwood Lodge became the overnight hostel for the crowds.

Denver's Rocky Mountain News chose "A Basin," as it came to be called, for a ski school directed by University of Denver coach Willy

Pee Wee Jones of Climax Ski Club at Winter Park, 1948. Starter, Jack Lindsey. #70 Eleanor Ganeug; #71 Rolf Dercum. Slalom races for children under age nine.

Schaeffler. In 1953, Arapahoe Basin hosted the first national giant slaloms for older citizens, and later Larry Jump and his wife, Marnie, were given a National Citizens' Award for developing Colorado's first amputee ski program. Jump built the first Poma lift in the nation at A Basin in 1954, and formed a corporation to market the relatively inexpensive disk–type tows, eventually selling to over 400 ski areas.

Not far away, Berthoud Pass opened the nation's first double chairlift in 1947. Special trains still ran from Denver to Winter Park, where hundreds of youngsters got their first ski experience. The ski school at Winter Park was conducted by Camp Hale veteran Harald "Pop" Sorensen, who started a jumping program sponsored by the *Denver Post*. In 1950, University of Colorado Coach Steve Bradley took over

An early well-dressed skier, 1939.

direction of Winter Park, constructing the Balcony House with solar heating, a radical novelty in those days, and inventing the Bradley Packer Grader to earn the title of "Father of Slope Maintenance."

At Leadville, Cooper Hill was shared with the army by Lake County people during the Korean War. Don Larsh, popular Western State College graduate, built up a fine youth ski program and introduced hundreds of adults to the sport. Close by, Jack Gorsuch was mentor at Climax, founding the careers of world competitors Scott and Rudd Pyles and Dave Gorsuch. A few miles down the Arkansas, Ray and Josephine Berry of Salida were developing Monarch Pass from T-bar to chairlift status.

Snow mania still reigned in Steamboat, with Al Wegeman's pioneer school team. Steamboat's high school band had marched on skis since 1936. In 1960, Marcellus Merrill, a Steamboat youth who jumped with Howelsen and Prestrud, was later a partner of Thor Groswold in Denver, designed the metal ski, patented the first American three-point binding for downhill, slalom, jumping, and cross-country, devised a car-top carrier, and generally won regard as Colorado's outstanding ski inventor.

Wegeman, who had earlier taught at Winter Park, established an outstanding record in the art of teaching. He left Steamboat to teach in Sun Valley in 1948, but died of cancer in 1950. Stepping into his bindings at Steamboat was Gordy Wren, often praised as the state's greatest all-around skier. After returning from Italy after the war, Wren went to Aspen, where he met and married the creative Jean Maxwell. Gordy scored well in the Olympics at St. Moritz in 1948, being the only American ever to qualify in all four competitions—downhill, slalom, jumping, and cross-country.

Wren took over at Steamboat with the elan Wegeman had fostered and polished off the techniques of many of the town's bumper crop of prize winners. That town's record is amazing: John Steele, first Colorado Olympian in 1932; Crosby Perry-Smith; Keith and Paul Wegeman;

Famous base house at Steamboat Springs' Howelsen Hill. Airborne view of many world champion jumpers.

Katy Rodolph; Buddy, Skeeter, and Loris Werner; Jon and Jere Elliot; Chris McNeil; Lonny Vanatta; Jeff Davis; Jim "Moose" Barrows; Marvin Crawford and his son, Gary; all noble heirs to the grand tradition established by Howelsen and Dalpe.

Wren moved to Reno, Nevada in 1956 to start a junior program there. He turned the keys to the Howelsen lift over to Rudy Schnackenberg, another Tenth Mountain instructor, who continued to produce winners. Aspen's financial coup moved Steamboaters to envision a great resort, and by the late fifties, Jim Temple, a Sun Valley ski patrolman, showed up and sensed the potential of Storm Mountain, towering over the town.

Other ventures, some under-financed and fated to die young, began the postwar decades. Some flourished. Hot Sulphur Springs had a new rush of interest with fresh facilities in 1947; Glen Cove re-equipped

Bob Carlson and Ned Wood of Denver having a bit of trouble developing their ski legs, 1948.
Charles Grover photo.

itself and Cripple Creek launched the Tenderfoot Mountain area. Hopeful developers opened up slopes at Hidden Park, Allenspark, and Indianhead. Silverton's Kendall Mountain was developed in 1961, and two million dollars were said to have been invested in Rollins Pass, the old railroad route to Middle Park. Squaw Pass had a tow, and the English-style ski hangout, The Coachman, was opened at Hideaway Park in 1963. In southern Colorado, Top O'La Veta was launched in 1959, and the old mining town of Creede installed a tow and toboggan run. Evergreen, near Denver, saw its plans for expansion dashed by cancellation of a federal loan in 1965, but would be the center of a later great debate as an Olympic site.

Fun Valley, a new area for intermediates, began operation up the Deer Creek Road at Denver's back door in 1968, while Westcliffe, beneath the towering Sangre de Cristo Ranch, struggled in isolation. East of Durango, Forest Lakes ski area was established, and on the state line south of Trinidad was Raton–Sugarite. Ouray had its own tow, and Stoner, north of Cortez, was a success on a small scale.

The big era of Colorado's massive resorts, however, opened with the decade that began in 1960.

TOP LEFT: Berthod Pass, 1938. Spring skiing in Colorado has always been a crazy time of year.

TOP RIGHT: Skiing Berthod Pass, Colorado. Early day skiers had lift lines just like today.

BOTTOM RIGHT: Amputee skiing started at Winter Park.

Steamboat's famous skiing band performing at Winter Carnival.

CHAPTER EIGHT

LEARNING HOW TO MINE SNOW

Colorado drawing boards were sagging with the weight of unbelievably ambitious plans for new resorts in the sixties.

Many older areas had added lifts in the waning fifties, and every year thousands of new skiers were drawn to Colorado slopes. In 1958, the fashionable Broadmoor Hotel near Colorado Springs hired Steve Knowlton to take over its ski program which had been a minor operation for decades. A new chairlift was added, and the frequent shortage of adequate snow made it one of the first spots in the state to augment Mother Nature with a Larchmount snow-making machine. At Hidden Valley, near Estes Park, plows kept part of Trail Ridge Road open for the slope which was popular with college clubs.

Colorado's uranium boom of the fifties sent thousands of people to the high country carrying Geiger counters on hikes, picnics, and even cross-country ski treks. In 1954, one such prospector, Earl V. Eaton, was climbing around his own Minturn territory when he gazed at what was later called Vail Mountain. Seeing it was the mother lode of the ski industry, he brought in Loveland Basin's manager, Pete Seibert, for a look-see, and Pete recognized the mountain for something more valuable than radioactive ore.

Within the next few years, the two formed a modest enterprise known as the Trans Montane Rod and Gun Club as a cover against wild land speculation and applied for a ski permit from the Forest Service. What grew up there, after major investments followed, would eventually become the continent's largest single skiing complex. Vail installed the first gondola lift in the nation, edging out Crested Butte in a race by a

Typical of local ski runs which gave little youngsters their start was this one at Cranor Hill, 1968.

matter of a month or so, and also put up two Riblet double chairlifts. The whole operation opened December 15, 1962, although it wasn't until Christmas Eve that the slopes got a present of a heavy snowstorm.

Vail has to be one of the most successfully promoted areas in the history of skiing. Some resort-watchers maintain that the advertising that went into it was as costly as the construction itself. Results count, and the results were magnificent. Seibert drew together a championship crew to lead the operation, including Hale companions "Sarge" Brown to lead the ski school and Robert Parker, editor of *Skiing* magazine, to publicize it into a name as well-known as Aspen. Parker knew how to draw celebrities and inspire magazine articles. Big money was soon stumbling over each other's ski poles to invest with names like Murchison, Sears

Cross-country ski hike mountains near Crested Butte. 1963.

Roebuck, Quaker Oats, Schlitz, Federated Stores, Upjohn, and even a few Colorado corporations. Gradually, the polyglot architecture, originally sort of an "Instant Tyrolia" style, filled up the whole valley with an East Vail, West Vail, and Beaver Creek. When enthusiast Gerald R. Ford became President Ford, the television cameras followed him to his winter vacations there.

Vail had been racing with two other major contenders, Crested Butte and Breckenridge, neither of which attracted as much wealth quite so quickly. Crested Butte was truly isolated compared to Vail, which was moved even closer to Denver with the construction of the Eisenhower Tunnel under Loveland Pass. However, the great snowfall at Crested Butte convinced three young Kansans, Dick Eflin, Fred Rice, and

Skijoring race at Steamboat Springs.

Tom Welch, to buy a ranch on the Butte and build a tow. Paul Panion engineered the first lift, while Skip Allen and Jim Prendergast started the ski school.

The Crested Butte team then decided to get into a gondola lift race with Vail. Prendergast sped to Houston for parts, and engineers from Italy showed up with a slightly used gondola. Local men and women kept dashing over to Vail to compare progress, but it wasn't until late January of 1963 that the Butte lift rolled. Crested Butte was a genuine mining town, retaining the flavor of its immigrant settlers from Slovenia and Italy. It was only appropriate that the gondola be blessed by the village padre, who stumbled and wrenched his knee during the ceremony, seen as a bit foreboding for the prospects of the new resort.

Nearby Western State College students flocked into the playground from Gunnison as new managers cultivated the trade, but being too isolated and under-advertised, Crested Butte entered the doors of bankruptcy several times. A few years later, Howard "Bo" Callaway and his brother-in-law, Ralph Walton, from prominent Georgia families, bought the operation and relative solvency emerged. There arose a second town, Mount Crested Butte, on the knee of the behemoth peak. Callaway became Secretary of the Army during the Ford Administration, and while he hoped to expand Crested Butte, in the fallout from Watergate, charges flowed that he was unduly influencing the Department of Agriculture's Forest Service to grant permits. He resigned as Ford's campaign manager to fight his antagonists. At nationally-televised hearings in Washington, Callaway emerged unscathed, and the tempests jumped out of the Crested Butte teapot in a hurry.

By the end of the seventies, the quaint Victorian town was shaken when AMAX, Inc., which had grown from Climax Molybdenum Company, discovered that Mount Emmons, locally known as the Red Lady, had in their words, "an elephant" of precious molybdenum inside its skin. A soaring economy made the steel-hardening mineral valuable, and many an old miner cheered to think a bonanza had come to Crested Butte

Hot Dog skiing at Steamboat Springs winter carnival ends in a benign plunge into a hot springs pool.

once more. The ski crowd, however, doing their own type of "mining," did not look upon the idea with joy, pointing to the Climax operation above Leadville, a controversial story in Colorado mining. AMAX responded that it had learned how to do the job with finesse, but as the battle boiled, some Crested Butte residents went so far as to light up the side of the Red Lady one night with another four-letter word over the letters "AMAX." National magazines covered the dispute, and mining preliminaries were under way when the national economy took a deep bow, and AMAX decided the project should be placed on "hold."

It was the waters of Lake Dillon, thirsty Denver's major water supply project, that stirred Breckenridge out of its doldrums into a new era of tourism, as summer visitors flocked to the tranquil new reservoir. John Bailey had built a tow on Cemetery Hill near the inundated old Dillon townsite in the late forties and then became involved with A Basin management. Breckenridge, nearby, was still remembered for the looming rocks left when the mighty floating monster gold dredge had headed down its main street, scooping up the upper Blue River, sorting the sands for pay dirt.

Bill Rounds, a Kansas vacationer, joined with Whip Jones of Aspen Highlands to see what could be done with Peak 8, overlooking the town. Their ensuing race with Vail posed problems for the Forest Service permit people, who considered the areas too close together. Keystone and Copper Mountain would crowd in even later. Vail protested the application, but Breckenridge promoters took the case to Washington, D.C., and by late 1961, the resort opened with a Heron double chairlift, a T-bar, and a restaurant. Aspen's Red Rowland came over to engineer the lift, and other skiing stars joined the staff. Harry Baum, Jr., of Denver, leased the resort for most of the sixties, and in 1969, Peak 9 was added to the offerings. Then, Aspen Ski Corporation bought the operation, appointing West Portal veteran John Rahm as manager. He was succeeded by James Art Bowles who built Colorado's first Alpine Slide there, a 2,600-foot dual-track sled run designed by

Demag of West Germany. In 1978, Aspen Ski Corporation and all of its subsidiaries merged with Twentieth Century Fox Film Corporation.

Among those Aspen subsidiaries was the Snowmass development which had taken a long time to emerge. In 1957, Fritz Benedict had spotted the Baldy Mountain–Burnt Mountain locale, about a dozen miles west of Aspen, and begun the paperwork. Bill Janss, a California investor, eventually brought in American Cement Corporation as his partner to fund $10 million worth of ski runs and lifts. To confuse old-timers and newcomers alike, the owners chose to name the resort Snowmass Village, to differentiate it from the old village of Snowmass, nearby on the main Aspen highway. As a further complication, the slope itself was called Snowmass-at-Aspen. With Stein Eriksen leading the ski school, its opening in 1967 proved a full success. Janss Corporation sold its share to American Cement which eventually sold it to Aspen Ski Corporation.

Steamboat Springs pro skier Lonny Vanatta.

At Steamboat Springs, Jim Temple had gained permits for a new Storm Mountain Corporation, formed with John Fetcher, a Harvard-educated local rancher; Gerald Groswold of the Denver ski family; famed local skiers Marvin Crawford and Buddy Werner; Denver's Bill Sayer; and Sam Huddleston, a Denver landscape architect. Fetcher, as president, became a model of local dedication as every autumn he mortgaged his cattle herd to keep the

Billy Kidd at Steamboat Springs.

construction going, and personally cannonballed his cattle truck to California to bring back a bull wheel for the double lift. Denver banks came to the rescue as construction costs threatened the dream, and Storm Mountain opened on January 12, 1963. The night before the big event, Steamboat's mercury shriveled to forty below, shattering plastic garbage cans and splitting plastic dashboards in cars all over town. Only five people showed up for the maiden voyage of the new lift!

Storm Mountain was later renamed Mount Werner after Steamboat's Buddy Werner, a very special name in the annals of Colorado competitors, being the first American to win a major European event, Austria's Hahnenkaam. Werner followed that with a string of victories, including collegiate skiing with the University of Colorado, U.S. National, Roch Cup, Harriman Cup, Gran Prix at Chamonix, and others. He was twice an Olympian and twice in the FIS meets.

On Sunday morning, April 12, 1964, Werner was skiing for a German camera crew filming Olympic contenders in Switzerland. It was a beautiful day, and the ballet rhythms of the sixteen skiers were to be accompanied on the finished film only by the sound of music. Suddenly,

Aspen, 1951.   Bud Livingston, Robert Smilanic, Bob Oberhide.

Robert Smilanic photo.

The Kids Hill Ski Run and rope tow in Telluride was built by the Idarado Mining Company and Telluride community in 1964. The cost of a lift ticket was only $5. Photo from the Homer Reid collection.

Billy Mahonoey, Sr. photo.

an avalanche thundered down, catching Buddy, who started to ski the surface but was buried nine feet under by a second avalanche triggered by the first. As the international skiing fraternity mourned the loss, Steamboat Springs flew flags at half-mast. A special trophy was established in his memory, the new library was named for him, and a youth program was established in several Colorado resorts.

Gordy Wren returned to Steamboat to manage Mount Werner after Marvin Crawford decided to enter the business world. Gordy had been in Wyoming managing the stupendous Jackson Hole development. Ling Temco Vought (LTV) Corporation bought Mount Werner in 1970 and added a gondola lift. A stellar staff of local greats led the ski school; new hotels and condominiums sprouted around the base, and Sven Wiik retired after two decades of coaching at Western State College to open a Scandinavian lodge and cross-country ski touring trail system. The original Colorado ski town had at last become big time.

Bob Sayer, another Camp Hale vet, took the leadership with the Grand Mesa Ski Corporation to develop Powderhorn near Grand Junction in 1966. With a chairlift in full operation, the slopes eeked out only 21,000 tickets the first season, but California investors came in to help, and patronage doubled a few years later.

Meanwhile, up at the Ski Tip Ranch under the Continental Divide, Max and Edna Dercum at last saw their resort, Keystone, open in 1970. To protect the terrain, towers of the lifts were "helicoptered" as high as the 11,640-foot summit. The simple lodge grew into a grand complex of restaurants, shops, and hotels, serving both Keystone and nearby Arapahoe Basin, together providing fifteen lifts. Ralston-Purina Corporation added Keystone to its cereal empire in 1975, but Max and Edna kept racing, winning several senior citizen kudos.

North of Durango, Chet Anderson, Forest Service weather expert, had the brainstorm to create Purgatory, with promotional support from Ray Duncan. Named from the Spanish term for the lost souls of the

Billy Mahoney Sr., laying it down at a Telluride ski race in 1941.

Billy Mahoney Sr. photo.

nearby Animas River, it thrived with an average snowfall of 300 inches, drawing numerous skiers in the late sixties from New Mexico and Arizona, as well as Colorado. Anderson headed mountain operations there, and John Briner directed the ski school. That fine old pioneer founder of Denver's Arlberg Club, Graeme McGowan, built the lodge. Dick Peterson, who had formerly led Vail Associates, later managed Purgatory in the tried and true Vail style. The next decade brought the luxurious Tamarron resort seven miles to the south, where Allen Small, of the American Biathlon (skiing and shooting) Team, set up a ski touring center.

In Glenwood Springs, where the original chair lift had been built on Red Mountain just in time to suffer from World War II travel restrictions, new directions were explored after the war. John Vanderhoof, who later became Colorado governor and then directed Colorado West's Club Twenty promotional organization, skied around the area with friends and located a new area, calling it Holliday Hill,

Upper Hughes at Winter Park, 1968.

Robert Smilanic photo.

later to become Sunlight. The Red Mountain area changed hands several times, but gradually slipped from operation as Chicago's John Riggs, a commercial artist, got investment fever and opened Sunlight in 1966. With other corporate financing, Sunlight grew gradually, and the management began to scan the adjoining Williams Peak slopes for expansion.

As these developments ebbed and flowed during the sixties, perhaps the most significant to Coloradans' personal lives were the tiny local slopes established at dozens of towns. Citizens strung ropes and then held bake sales to purchase Poma or J-bar lifts to give their youths a chance to ski inexpensively. Gunnison's Cranor Hill, Dallas Divide for the Montrose–Ouray crowd, Fawn Valley above Paonia; the list could be extended even to embrace the Great Plains of eastern Colorado. Gradually skiing became a respectable sport in high schools and one of the most popular of all in the colleges and universities of the state.

Skiing down the Oh-Be-Joyful Run at Mount Crested Butte.

University of Colorado's Karl Busk in an NCAA jumping meet. Phot by Kristen Rudd.
Colorado Ski Museum/Hall of Fame photo.

CHAPTER NINE

SLATE BOARDS AND SKI WAX

When the Steamboat Springs school board opened the gate to student skiing in 1943, they started other state schools on the downhill trail to education of better skiers and more people involved in a lifelong recreation. By 1956, nine other schools had taken the jump: Aspen, Colorado Rocky Mountain School at Carbondale, Durango, Hayden, Hot Sulphur Springs, Leadville, Climax, Middle Park, and Telluride.

Institutions of higher education had active ski clubs in the thirties, with informal competition among them. James L. Harsh pioneered the ski club at Colorado A & M. (later Colorado State University). There were also clubs at the University of Denver, University of Colorado, Colorado College, Adams State, Mesa, Colorado School of Mines, and Western State. Highest in elevation, Western had the earliest program, dating from 1916.

World War II eclipsed club activities, but V-J Day saw a great resurgence of enthusiasm. Colorado State College at Greeley formed a club, as did Otero, Pueblo, Regis, and Trinidad colleges. Edward Taylor, founder of the original organized club at Mines, helped establish intercollegiate skiing competition in the mountain states, as well as the National Ski Patrol. He was the first Coloradoan to be inducted into the National Ski Hall of Fame.

Gradually, the clubs gained sanction as teams. Intercollegiate skiing became a national enterprise when Physical Education Director Paul W. "Frosty" Wright at Western State, fought all the way through the conservatism of the National Collegiate Athletic Association to establish skiing as an official sport in 1954.

The children of Hahn's Peak School in Steamboat Springs enjoy the snow in 1914, just like kids today.

Bob Beattie, famed ski coach at the University of Colorado and a founder of big-time pro skiing.

Earliest of the regular ski teams to emerge were Colorado A & M, Colorado College, and Colorado School of Mines. Later, the Air Force Academy sent competitors to the meets. The real powerhouses of the sport, however, were the University of Denver, the University of Colorado, Fort Lewis College in Durango, and Western State.

Steve Bradley coached the C.U. team from its formation in the forties until he took over Winter Park in the early fifties. He was succeeded by Tom Jacobs, later secretary of the National Ski Association. Skiing really took off at C.U., however, in 1957, when Bob Beattie came from Middlebury College in Vermont and led the Buffaloes to the National Collegiate (NCAA) crowns in 1959 and 1960. By 1963, his powerhouse team included Buddy Werner, Jim Huega, Bill Marolt, and Barbara Ferries. (Individual records of many collegiate champions are included in Appendix I.)

Beattie became head coach for the United States alpine teams, leading the nation's participation in four FIS and two Olympic meets. He left the University of Colorado in 1965 for the United States alpine team coaching position and later moved to Aspen, where he promoted professional skiing. He was a founding father of the World Cup Races, a commissioner of NASTAR recreational skiing, and author of a significant national guide to ski racing. Gordi Eaton and M. J. Elisha took hands at coaching the Buffaloes until 1967, when two students, Jim Hoeschler and Mike Rommine, kept the university in competition with the encouragement of Dean Steve Romine.

Sven Wiik, patriarch of modern Colorado cross-country skiing and former coach at Western State College.

Colorado Ski Museum/Hall of Fame photo.

National wins returned to C.U. in 1969 when it hired Bill Marolt, its alumnus and international champ. As coach, he led the team to a cornucopia of crowns from the NCAA from 1972 through 1979, when the nation called him to lead Olympic contenders. Another former Buff, Tim Hinderman, grasped the poles and put the Boulder boys into national championships again by 1982.

Colorado's pioneer championship team, however, was that of the University of Denver with its famed coach, Willy Schaeffler. An Austrian draftee into Hitler's army, Schaeffler became an undercover resistance fighter against the Nazis and was caught in one of his adventures, barely escaping the firing squad. Finally reaching the

The snow is up to the eaves of the house at Grand Mesa but everyone (including the dog) is having fun in 1922.

United States after the war, Schaeffler was hired as ski coach at the University of Denver, where he compiled a stunning record, turning out thirteen national championships. Peter Pytte spelled Willy while the master directed the 1960 Squaw Valley Olympic ski events and later succeeded him to grab a few more national firsts.

Regarded by many as Colorado's greatest ski promoter, Schaeffler revolutionized instruction with his advocacy of the Wedeln technique of

short turns amid a storm of controversy among instructors. He launched
the ski school at A Basin and helped set up the handicapped program
there. He was later United States alpine director, establishing an
official training center at Park City, Utah in 1974.

While the two universities garnered the national titles, they usually had
to edge past pace-setting Western State College, a small liberal arts
school. It was Colorado's real ski school, along with a fine educational

Upper Hughes at Winter Park in 1968. It's always nice to have the sun out and great new snow. Robert Smilanic photo.

offering, and probably accounted for the growth of skiing as recreation in the state through its production of quality coaches more than any other institution.

Sven Wiik, Western's original coach, was a native of Sollefetea, Sweden. Wiik came to America in 1949 and began writing to various ski areas for an instruction job. Western wasn't on his list, but ski manufacturer Thor Groswold, an Arapahoe Basin investor, saw the letter. Groswold had two sons at Western and interested the college in hiring Wiik. Torn between an offer from Lake Placid, New York, and Colorado, Sven chose the latter and launched a program which changed the history of the mountain college. When he left there for the Steamboat country, Sven, who had been U. S. Olympic Nordic coach, established a ski touring center which would break the trail for a full revival of cross-country as an alternative to downhill in Colorado. His successor at Western was Kenneth MacLennan, a former student. Another of Wiik's champs had been Adolph Kuss, who became coach at Fort Lewis College, turning out other championships for that school.

The growth of intercollegiate skiing peaked at the beginning of the seventies. Within the next decade, both the University of Denver and Fort Lewis found they could no longer afford the financial pressure of intercollegiate teams. University of Colorado had, however, dominated the college ski world for three decades, giving succor to many international champions and sending skilled instructors throughout the nation.

With scholastic skiing on the decline, the resort business was still booming with a proliferation of new areas and expansion of existing resorts that made the sport a major income producer in Colorado by 1980. Much of this activity was ignited by Olympic fever – the hope that Denver would be the site of the 1976 Winter Olympics.

Ellen Stewart and Ann Altemus at Dallas Divide, at the foot of Mt. Sneffels, 1984.

Doug Stewart photo.

CHAPTER TEN

THE STRANGE CASE
OF THE ALMOST OLYMPICS

For decades, some of Colorado's leaders had looked forward to a day when Denver would host the Winter Olympics. By 1967, a committee had been formed to present a bid for the contests to be held in 1976, Colorado's centennial year of statehood. Many citizens glowed with satisfaction, thinking it would be a simple matter to house the crowds in Denver and run special trains to Winter Park, the seemingly logical site for daily events.

From time to time, a few critics pointed out that Olympics, like World Fairs, often proved financial disasters for host cities, but arguments for winter tourism promotion usually overrode those carping comments. Perhaps the committee had overdrawn the picture it painted of Denver's proximity to ski areas when it persuaded Olympic officials to approve the site. In any event, doubts gradually clouded the scene.

When the foothills town of Evergreen, with its variable climate and unpredictable snowfall, was named for cross-country events, residents rose in opposition. Other Coloradans wondered about strange schemes creeping into the planning. Real estate promoters were talking about whole new ski areas to be built with federal and state funds. Environmentally concerned citizens dreaded the prospect of "cardboard cities" erected to house the visitors.

The U. S. Forest Service suggested Copper Mountain's setting just east of Vail as the best Olympic site, but some laymen pondered the fact that there were no existing ski tows there. Vail wanted to develop Beaver Creek at nearby Avon. Traditionalists pushed for Steamboat Springs, but it was a long commute from Denver.

Cross-country skiing on Red Mountain Pass, 1984.

Doug Stewart photo.

Estimates of costs soared and soured. The earliest figure of $14 million quickly shot up to $25 million. Someone noted that the 1968 games cost Grenoble $250 million, and that Sapporo, Japan, was raising $750 million for the 1972 games. (These later figures included much civic revamping not directly related to the games.) Transportation and housing quagmires loomed large on the tongues of opponents. Who was going to get a free resort built by the taxpayers? Who was going to build new roads or design super-buses for existing highways? Answers were not clear in coming. Denver newspapers alternately froze and thawed on the issue, with varying swings of public opinion adding to the chaotic public relations headaches of the Denver Olympic Committee.

At Sapporo in 1972, Olympic officials received a surprise visit by a delegation from the Citizens for Colorado's Future, a group opposed to the Colorado site. The presentation the group made focused world-wide publicity on the squabble, and led to the temporary withdrawal of Denver by the officials. The "coup de grace" came in November of 1972, when both Colorado and Denver city voters overwhelmingly approved measures which would ban any further expenditure of public funds for the Olympics, a drive spearheaded by State Representative Bob Jackson of Pueblo. The site was switched to Innsbruck, Austria.

Frustrations exploded, with charges and counter-charges over the loss or gain to Colorado's image as a ski country. Politicians emerged with platforms pointing out their contributions to both the economic and environmental salvation of the state, and many won elections on the issue. The Olympic plans, however, were never forgotten, and some Coloradans were talking seriously of a later Olympic invitation.

There were those who hoped, and others who feared, that Colorado's growth in winter sports would level off after the Olympic fiasco. Olympics or not, new ski areas appeared all through the seventies.

Towering over Wheeler Flats, a few miles west of Dillon, was Copper Mountain, a natural choice for a major ski area which had been mentioned in the Olympic package. Charles D. "Chuck" Lewis, former

Nora Chandler cuts a path through the fresh snow at Red Mountain Pass.
Doug Stewart photo.

Vail executive, joined Charles Froelicher, headmaster of the Colorado Academy in Denver, to promote financing of the new venture. Lured to the Olympic prospect were the heirs of the McCormick farm equipment estate and several other Colorado resort speculators. Despite the defeat of the games, the resort opened in 1973 to enjoy a profitable and growing reputation. Lewis remained at the helm until 1981, when he sold Copper Mountain to Apex Petroleum Company.

Another major resort, Telluride, gained its start in the early seventies. People in the old and famed San Juan mining town had skied for decades. Joe Zoline, a wealthy enthusiast, became godfather of the slopes there, and spectacular new runs were baptized by the boards in 1972.

Nora Chandler touring above timberline, 1984.

Doug Stewart photo.

Vail, jammed by the mid–seventies, reached out downstream to the town of Avon, another Olympic speculation, to promote the Beaver Creek area. The plan ran into a sitzmark–strewn trail, as doubts arose over environmental damage and the extension of the string of condominiums for another ten miles along the scenic valley. Despite delayed Forest Service sanctions, Governor John Vanderhoof expressed concern over a thousand fireplaces smoking up the valley. His successor, Richard D. Lamm, tried to block the project, and Senator Gary Hart asked the Forest Service to review its decision. Vail's tactful Robert Parker maintained the tenacity to carry on, answering each charge as it arose throughout the latter half of the decade, and it slowly evolved into reality, with ex–President Gerald Ford being a major purchaser of land there.

Ski tourers on Sven Wiik's trails at Steamboat Springs.

Beaver Creek opened at last in 1980. As time went on, Goliad Oil Company gained control of Vail, along with the Beaver Creek expansion.

Farther down the valley at Eagle, the Adam's Rib ski area plan did not fare so well. There was local opposition and the Aspen interests, just across the ridge from the huge area, fought it. While stymied in the permit stage by Governor Lamm's moratorium on new massive ski resorts in 1976, the process of permits and funding continued into the nineties, when the plan met its final death.

Meanwhile, the famed quarry town of Marble, surrounded by spectacular peaks, had lain dormant since the exciting days in which it produced stone for such graceful edifices as the Lincoln Memorial. Construction of a ski area there was underway, and lots were being sold, when hopes were shattered by the realization that it had an unstable terrain with landslides posing a constant threat. Many investors lost their money in what became "the Marble Bubble."

Other resorts which rose and fell during those years were Guanella Pass, Statecoach near Steamboat, and Steamboat Lake near Hahn's Peak. Above Ashcroft, plans for a grand Montezuma Basin resort were abandoned, and other dreams faded after enthusiastic starts.

In spite of the touchy issue of conservation and the wildly inflated construction costs of that time, other small areas did open. Stoner, north of Cortez, grew, and Hesperus, west of Durango, offered an inexpensive ski site for beginners. One of the most unexpected locations for skiing was Sharktooth, six miles west of Greeley. Down on the plains, it served a simple 150-foot drop with a thousand-foot ski tow. Ski Idlewild wedged into the Winter Park vicinity as a family resort, and Silver Creek, near Granby, opened with two triple chairlifts and one double chairlift. The owners of Silver Creek have recently purchased the Berthoud Pass area. Ski Golden on Lookout Mountain and Arapahoe East in Mount Vernon Canyon were both convenient to Denverites. Near Ute Pass, west of Colorado Springs, commuters could go to an improved Pikes Peak area.

Ellen Stewart and Bob Borchert ski into the gathering storm atop Grand Mesa.
Doug Stewart photo.

In southern Colorado, the eastern slopes of the mighty Sangre de Cristo Mountain range afforded deep snow for three new projects. Cuchara, near La Veta, opened in 1982, boasting 265 inches of snow as average for its Baker Mountain slopes. San Isabel attracted family skiing. Conquistador, near Westcliffe, grew to a multiple chairlift operation under the guidance of Richard Milstein. While removed from the Denver metro area as compared to other sites, these areas appeal to plains states skiers, especially those with an aversion to crossing high mountain passes.

Above all, these more modest areas brought Colorado skiing back into the budgets of many who felt that the sport was becoming practical only for financial kings. While perhaps the earliest days of two dollar bunks and fifty-cent tows were long gone, many families could enjoy the fun without flirting with bankruptcy. Thousands found they could forego the purple luxury of so many of the nationally-famed resorts. For many skiers, the smaller hosts provided adequate challenge to suit skiing abilities.

Much of the promotional credit for Colorado's resort success must go to the dedicated leadership of an organization known as Colorado Ski Country USA. Likewise, credit for identifying and preserving the heritage is due Vail's tasteful Colorado Ski Museum and Hall of Fame.

Ski Country USA was formed in 1963, as a result of an idea session of the Southern Rocky Mountain Ski Area Operators Association, although Vail had previously used the name. Steve Knowlton was the first executive director, giving a dynamic beginning on which Tod Martin and R. Garrett Mitchell were later to build. Colorado Ski Country USA led a drive to get the state into cloud seeding during the snow drought of 1976-1977, and it produced promotional slide shows for national circulation. It worked with the Forest Service on RARE (Roadless Area Review and Evaluation) studies and monitored such issues as the "liability crunch" which increased costs of lift tickets by making operators liable for skier injuries under some circumstances. Georgia Lodders, the area operational director, served the organization for more than two decades. As interests in winter sports broadened, so did the scope of operation, with an expansive marketing effort and coordination among all member resorts.

Robert W. Parker was a principal founder of the Colorado Ski Museum and Hall of Fame, founded in 1976 as a non-profit historical organization supported by gifts and memberships. Each year it chooses notable contributors to Colorado skiing for induction into the Hall of Fame. Donald Simonton was its first curator. Beautifully displayed exhibits at the Vail museum are open and free to the public. A statewide board of directors represents diverse ski interests, and with several ski writers, chooses the new Hall of Fame honorees each spring. Steamboat Springs' Tread of the Pioneers Museum also has a fine collection of skiing history, as does Aspen's Stoddard House.

Greg Simpson just before wiping out.

CHAPTER ELEVEN

GETTING A LIFT AND
SHOOTING DOWN POWDER

Sport skiing was never considered when the United States Government established the national forests nearly a century ago. Mining, lumbering, grazing, fishing, and hunting were to be kept in balance on the fifth of Colorado lands reserved for national forests. In addition to this, the federal government held national parks and huge blocks of less forested lands administered by the Bureau of Land Management.

It was on the national forests that most of the ski resorts would be located. Nine Colorado forests, more than thirteen million acres of mountainous terrain, were under the supervision of the U.S. Forest Service. Ultimately, snow would emerge as the forests' most precious product, watering the West through four major river systems and fostering the huge income generated by the ski industry.

In the first stages of Colorado skiing, foresters welcomed the jolly slatsmen and cheered when they helped construct the crude tows of the thirties. After World War II, the Forest Service faced a multitude of propositions and gradually became a key factor in the design of new winter sports areas. Sprawling far beyond the ranches or mining claims on which they started, ski areas climbed mountains which could set off mighty avalanches when trails cut into the natural vegetation. Ski runs could cut off wild animal trails, lure smog, invade scenic views, shrink grazing land, disturb fishing waters, veto mining projects, jam firefighters' roads, annihilate nesting grounds, and shatter the tranquillity sought by outdoor lovers. On the other hand, never would so many people make so much use of the forests as when they went there to ski.

Every beginner should suffer the problems of a rope tow before the luxury of a lift. Photographed by John Briner, Dean of Colo. ski school directors.

The discrete placement of areas became a necessity, giving rise to the true "snow rangers," specialists in dealing with such problems. Every forest had its experts working with designers and developers. These were the shock troops of the ski boom, and their decisions were not always welcome. Some controversies, such as Bo Callaway's proposed Snodgrass Mountain expansion of Crested Butte, became featured stories in national news. Still other decisions came a bit late, as in the case of the Marble ski area, after many had invested heavily in real estate based on resort values, only to find that the mountain loved to slide.

Paul Hauk was a notable example of the snow ranger, having one of the most extensive concentrations of ski area developments in his assignment, the White River National Forest. He was an expert in avalanche control, lift placement, and trail layout. His surveys became models of careful planning.

Because of an early snow, children practice skiing at home-waiting for the ski areas to open.
Robert Smilanic photo.

Avalanche control was a major problem, with the horrifying "white death" always a threat. Systematic cannon bombardment of snow ledges to set off slides before they flowed became the most common form of control. In another tactic, daredevil ski patrols planted dynamite charges to be exploded from what was hoped to be a safe distance. It was always dangerous work. In the spring of 1984, three patrol members were killed in an avalanche at Aspen Highlands which had been so triggered. In spite of all these precautions, slides continue to snuff out some lives in designated areas. Better discipline of downhill area skiers has helped reduce the toll, and now the threat is mostly to cross–country explorers on lonely trails away from the main slopes.

Along with better control of the slides themselves, search methods have improved with trained rescuers more likely to locate victims before they expire. Skier education has led to better survival chances for those caught in catastrophic cascades. While always a danger, avalanches do not pose the appalling threat they did before experience taught its lethal lessons. Ski patrols realized that such disasters are neither inevitable nor necessarily fatal.

Too much snow in one place was a cause for consternation, but too little snow was a financial disaster. While areas in marginal climate, such as the Broadmoor in Colorado Springs, were among the first to install snow-making equipment, high mountain resort operators felt secure that it would always snow. Unlike farmers, they could not conceive of a crop loss now and then. Dendrochronologists, scientists who study tree ring growth patterns, could predict drought cycles. Severe ones came about every forty years, with lesser dry spells more frequent. Although the relationship is not fully understood, sunspot activity studies indicated similar cycles. Historians, who noted Colorado droughts in the late 1850s, the 1890s, and the 1930s, agreed with the scientists that the 1970s looked dubious.

Many in the ski industry, however, scorned the "gloom-mongering" academics, opening new shops and restaurants, blissfully mortgaged on the trust of inevitable snowfall. Infant that it was, the entire commercial ski business of the Rockies had never been through a severe drought. A minor dip in snowfall came in the early sixties just as Vail and Crested Butte were opening, but then the depths improved. The major drought hit about on schedule in the winter of 1976–1977, when Colorado areas took a loss of $78 million. There was a relapse in 1980–1981. Chartered planes landed near resorts, discharging ski-clad passengers from Dallas or Atlanta who were dismayed to find the ground bare during Christmas week. A few of the major areas had installed expensive snow-makers, but most went all-out after the lean years of snow. Now snow-making is a vital necessity in the ski area business. These remarkable systems consisted of little more than nozzle heads with mixes of air and water that had to be just right for creation of snow at slightly below freezing.

Marti Martin-Kuntz of Telluride, a champion speed skier who won the world record.
Jeff Andrew photo.

An even broader program involved the development of whole snowstorms through placement of silver iodide machines to shoot microscopic crystals into clouds from moisture condensation. The massive measures were controversial, having begun with concern for water in the thirsty West. The problem rested on proof that the snow which fell was indeed created by weather modification. Evidence favored the cloud seeders, but that stirred concern over disrupted mining and ranching operations from too much snow. Colorado as a state first took part in the ventures in 1951, and by 1977–1978, used emergency appropriations to place equipment on all mountain massifs over 9,500 feet in elevation. The ski areas benefited, although water supply was the main motivation.

Ten-man gainer, Crested Butte, 1975. Mark Perry photographed this longest combination flip ever made at that time.

Doug Stewart photo.

The Bradley Packer Grader, invented by the "Father of Slope Maintenance," Steve Bradley of Winter Park.
Colorado Ski Museum/ Hall of Fame photo.

Getting to the top of the runs is a story in itself in the history of skiing. Lifts came in a multitude of sizes, shapes, and concepts. While the first trams were the miners' buckets on cables sweeping over mountainsides, the first tourist lift was probably a 1907 gondola lift, the Sunrise Peak Aerial Tramway at Silver Plume.

Ski lifts had to wait until such inventions as boat tows in the mid–thirties. Crude as they were, they had advantages over mere rope tows. The first chairlift was the homemade job at the Pioneer area north of Gunnison in 1938.

Real progress came with the postwar boom days. Surface tows included T–bars, J–bars, and disk lifts. E. G. Comstam, who had been a fellow student of Albert Einstein, invented the T–bar and personally installed the longest one at the time at Camp Hale during the war. T–bars were the most expensive of surface lifts, followed by J–bars, and then the relatively affordable disk lifts.

Aerial tramways in Colorado started with single chairs and graduated through double and triple chairs, with Breckenridge installing the nation's first detachable quad lift in 1981. The first gondola lifts, at Vail and Crested Butte, were heralded for protection from wind when they started operation in the 1962–1963 season. Unlike Squaw Valley or Sandia, Colorado still awaits its first cable car tramway.

All told, Colorado's safety record has been outstanding, despite a tragic accident at Vail's Lionshead gondola in March of 1976, which killed four passengers and injured eight. All areas now have stringent monitoring plans to check the cable and lift conditions on a continuous basis. Most ski deaths are attributable to misjudgment and lack of awareness on the part of the victims. Some areas have now instituted "safety patrols" to help educate the public on how to be a responsible and respectful user of the slopes.

Forest Service monitoring of the lifts was an important function. Charles Dwyer, who had been an engineer with Heron Engineering and Ketchum, Konkel, and Hastings, two major builders in Colorado, brought a wealth of detailed knowledge to his job. He became Chief Aerial Tramway Engineer for the Forest Service in 1966, and had a major role in the establishment of the American National Standard for Passenger Tramways, writing a definitive book on the topic. In a rare move for government regulators, Dwyer began shifting responsibility for good engineering and safety to the private sector, as experience and skill have developed in the construction industries.

More skiers of recent years have been scorning the ski lifts for cross-country treks, helicopter lifts, and other innovations. These new directions have added even more to what has become one of Colorado's leading sources of income.

Telluride from the slopes, 1982.

Chapter Twelve

On Top of it All

In days of yore, skiers often ended the day sitting around a fireplace and singing songs together, perhaps with a glass of beer. The lodges were too far removed from good radio reception to allow electronics to disturb creative impulses. They loved such songs as "Two Boards Upon the Cold Powder Snow" and "Oola, Ski-Yumper from Norway." When things got dull, there were always practical jokes, such as the one in which Paul Hauk's companions waxed his skis with peanut butter after he had skied too quickly for them to follow.

Today the weary skier, after a day on shaped skis and well groomed trails, will relax in a hot tub while listening to cable music and order a cocktail from room service. The apres–ski scene, along with the snow sports experience, has merged into new altitudes of sophistication and technology.

Better equipment, grooming and trail planning, have reduced the once ever–present anxieties over spiral leg fractures, although knee injuries still claim their fair share of victims each season. Skiing and snow sports in general are far safer and more accessible that ever before.

There has been no end to the creativity applied toward new ways to enjoy skiing as we've progressed from hot–dogging, to freestyle, to aerials and now the extreme off–piste challenges, (off trail–back country) pushing the limits of athletic coordination and strength. Aspen's Stein Eriksen pioneered aerial flips and layouts during the fifties. The artistry grew into systematic classifications – clowning mogul runs, stunt and ballet forms, and aerial acrobatics. During the next decade, beautiful demon-strations of magic in the air and dancing on the snow became common

The torchlight Skiers of Telluride's Coonskin Carnival descend The Faces at night, a streak of fire through the trees.

sights on the slopes, but serious accidents with horrible injuries led to safety standards, introduced by the International Freestyle Skiers Association. Other groups protested the limits, bolting the organization. Steamboat Springs built a freestyle training jump over a warm swimming pool so that the acrobats could have a benign splash upon landing.

Another thrilling variation is speed skiing, in which the ultimate in air flow design of clothes and equipment are combined with perfect posture to reach velocities over 200 miles per hour. Contests of extreme skiing, moguls, snowboarding, telemarking and even snowbiking are held each season at most Colorado resorts.

There has also been a revival of cross-country treks, following the trails that had been broken by early mail carriers and miners. With thin boards and boundless energy, thousands have embraced backcountry skiing, venturing into wooded regions which had been the exclusive

Backcountry skiing in the Sneffles Range, 1997, using the San Juan Hut System.
Greg Simpson photo.

domain of wildlife during frozen months. Old–timers in towns all over the mountains fondly point back to the days of real skiing, and the revival has led to ski touring centers at most resorts. Sven Wiik of Steamboat Springs is generally regarded as the state's "Grand Patriarch" of this revival. The touring aspect has led to special designations away from resorts, too. United States Olympic Biathlon contender John Burritt laid out a trail system among the spectacular ridges and frozen lakes atop Grand Mesa. In 1984, the Crag Crest Trail was opened nearby and designated by the Forest Service as the first "National Ski Trail." The Tenth Mountain Trail Association, led by veteran Fritz Benedict, has been establishing a string of overnight huts on its trail through the Hunter–Fryingpan Wilderness Area northeast of Aspen.

Affluent adventurers can now hire helicopters to whisk them to pinnacles for the longest of runs in coveted untracked powder. A few daring souls

The Victorian village of Crested Butte is a National Historic Site.

Dan Peha photo.

have blended skydiving or hang gliding with skiing; others have raced in hot air balloons, sailing for a while before returning to the slats. The "Pole, Plod, Peddle and Paddle Races" down from Monarch Pass through Salida included skiing, running, bicycling, and ending up in a kayak contest through the spring floods of the Arkansas River. At Arapahoe and Lake Dillon, spring brings combinations of skiing and sailing.

By the end of the 1990s Colorado had recorded more than 52 million skier visits in a single winter and the industry accounted for over 3.2 billion dollars in revenue to the state. During the last decade of the century, the number of skiers flattened, as the baby boom generation aged and competition for the leisure dollar increased. As of 1999, Colorado had twenty-six developed ski resorts supporting over 66,000 jobs. The snow sports business remains the single biggest industry on the Western Slope.

Perhaps most favorable about this growth, in the minds of residents, was the fact that it was originally environmentally more desirable than heavy industry as an expansion of the economic base. There were problems, of course. The stretch along Interstate 70 to the major ski resorts is now one of the most congested commutes in Colorado, with bumper to bumper traffic on weekends. Ski industry planners have considered a variety of solutions to ease the traffic dilemma but so far no long term solution has been forthcoming.

Colorado resorts have begun to seriously court the international market and about six percent of the skiers come from other countries. The three top sources of international visitors are Canada, United Kingdom and Australia. Several larger resorts have expanded their marketing programs into non-English speaking regions, notably South America and Europe. Along with these efforts, multi-lingual signage and staffing have been an important and challenging goal to attract the lucrative international market.

Some of the nation's highest income and education levels were recorded by the counties of Pitkin (Aspen), Summit (A Basin, Breckenridge,

Copper, Keystone), Eagle (Vail, Beaver Creek), and Gunnison (Crested Butte). On the other hand, no resort towns have escaped the problems of drug and alcohol abuse, water supply issues, infrastructure strains, education challenges, and law enforcement shortages, as they deal with the social implications of a transient population and tourist economy. There is also a growing rift between the working class "locals" and the exploding number of wealthy homeowners, who frequent their "starter castles" for a few weeks of the year. Adequate and affordable housing for employees has become a major issue. Many resorts now consider the dilemma of attracting and housing their staff as the biggest challenge they face.

The nineties saw consolidation within the ski industry as never before. Many smaller ski areas went under and larger ski areas became part of corporate conglomerates which have diversified into real estate and summer recreation. As of 1999, some of the largest Colorado resorts are owned by North America's top three ski consortiums: Vail Resorts, Inc. which includes Vail, Keystone, Beaver Creek, and Breckenridge; American Skiing Company who owns Steamboat; and Intrawest who took over Copper Mountain. Many forecasters felt this trend would have a negative impact on the skiing consumer, but in fact, competition has remained healthy, as evidenced by the "season pass wars" where Coloradoans were offered an unrestricted pass for as low as $200! There is still a viable market as well for the smaller "feeder" resorts which, are often an ideal environment for beginners and a popular alternative to the mega resort atmosphere. The smaller resorts in Colorado are known as the "Gems of the Rockies," and they combine their marketing and sales efforts for out-of-state promotions. Isolated, rustic lodges that can be reached only by snow vehicle or on skis in the winter, are gaining popularity as people increasingly look for the solace of a true wilderness adventure. Irwin Lodge, an old mining site west of Crested Butte, is a prime example of these backcountry retreats.

The label of "ski area" has become obsolete as snowboarding, telemarking, ski boarding, etc, have become alternative ways to slide down the slopes. Many resorts have added skating, sleigh rides, snowmobiling, luge runs, history tours, snowshoeing, snowcat tours, ice show festivals and hockey games to their menu of winter activities. An increasing number of non-skiers are now vacationing in ski country, attracted by the history and beauty of the mountains in winter.

Despite the many changes, though, some customs survive through the decades. One is the venerable winter carnival. While Hot Sulphur Springs had the first, Steamboat Springs has the oldest continuous festival, now over eighty years of a blend of rich traditions in an exciting potpourri of winter fun. Carl Howelsen would probably be delighted if he could return to view the celebration he started, with its annual championship jumping platforms, bump and splash contests, and the "lighted man," who glides down a darkened hill with electric light bulbs dotting his body, skis, and poles. This is one of the world's strangest sights.

Most resorts have their equivalent share of winter madness and celebration, and those threads of tradition tie Colorado skiing, with its echoes of mining camp races, ski club outings, and old rustic lodges, to the present. In Aspen, they call it "Winterskol," at Crested Butte, it's "Flauschink," and at Winter Park, it's "Spring Splash," the final goodbye to winter. True enthusiasts, though, keep close watch of the weather map until Mother Nature drops her beloved powder, and the "Norwegian snowshoes" make fresh tracks on the virgin snow once again.

Appendix I: Who Did What?

This list includes men and women who made notable achievements in the history of Colorado skiing. No such list is ever complete, as many dedicated people were not given adequate recognition for their accomplishments. For explanations of awards, contests, and organizations, please refer to Appendix III.

The following abbreviations are used in the listing below:

CMC - Colorado Mountain Club

CSC-USA - Colorado Ski Country USA

CSHF - Colorado Ski Hall of Fame Inductee

CU - University of Colorado

DU - University of Denver

FIS - Federation Internationale de Ski

NASTAR - National Standard Ski Races

Nat. - National

NCAA - National Collegiate Athletic Association

NSHF - National Ski Hall of Fame Inductee

SRMSA - Southern Rocky Mountain Ski Association

10th Mt. Div. - Tenth Mountain Division, U. S. Army

USFS - United States Forest Service

WSC - Western State College

X-C - Cross-country

Aas, Morton. DU NCAA X-C champion, 1974.

Abbott, David. Chairman, Winter Sports, CMC 1932; original tournament committee, SRMSA.

Abbott, Dudley. One of original founders, Colorado Ski Museum and Hall of Fame; later president of board.

Adgate, Cary. CU NCAA champion, 1972; Olympian, 1976.

Ahern, Pat. Breckenridge Olympian jumper and X-C.

Aitken, Leonard. Early member of Arlberg Ski Club.

Allen, "Skip." Original ski instructor at Crested Butte.

Anderson, Chet. USFS weather expert; one of original developers of Purgatory ski area.

Armstrong, John. Mail carrier killed on ski run over Mosquito Pass in early 1860s.

Arnold, Landis. Tabernash Olympian jumper, 1984.

Arstal, Henning. DU NCAA All-American, 1957.

Ashley, Frank. Early Arlberg Club member; first president of SRMSA; mountain manager at Aspen; CSHF.

Atwater, Monty. Author of first avalanche handbook.

Baar, Ron. National Gelande champion, 1974.

Baar, Myke. Aspen jr. Champion; DU NCAA downhill champion, 1962.

Bailey, John. Former Brown University skier who built rope tow near old Dillon townsite in late 1940s; later director, instructor, and manager at Arapahoe Basin. Baker, Jim. Mountain guide whose use of skis is earliest documented in Colorado, 1857.

Balch, Bob. Original member of SRMSA classification committee; laid out original Winter Park trails; killed in action with 10th Mt. Div. In World War II; CSHF.

Balfanz, John. U.S. Olympic team; U.S. and North American Champion, best record of any American ski jumper in history. CSHFK.

Bancroft, Albert. Pioneer in early CMC skiing, Denver.

Banks, Jon. Vernal, Utah; "lighted man" in annual Steamboat Springs Winter Carnival.

Barrows, Jim "Moose." Nat. jumping champion from Steamboat Springs; CU winner of 1964 Schoenberger Award; FIS three times; 1971 pro "top ten;" president International Ski Racers Association, 1973; instructor, Steamboat Springs. CSHF.

Barwise, Norman. Early Arlberg Club member; first to ride first Colorado ski tow, Berthoud, 1936.

Bass, Harry. Chairman, Vail Associates, helped develop Vail and Beaver Creek.

Baum, Harry J. Denver businessman who leased and operated Breckenridge, 1960s.

Bayer, Herbert. Famed design specialist who managed Paepcke's original Aspen Ski Corporation.

Bayer, Seth. CU NCAA champion, giant slalom, 1982; Schoenberger Award, 1981.

Beattie, Bob. CU coach; head coach US Alpine team, 1962-68; coach US Olympic and FIS teams; Commissioner for NASTAR; winner of Blegen Plaque, Golden Quill; first American Bell Award; originated concept of pro circuit and helped found World Cup races; author of Guide to Ski Racing; CSHF; NSHF.

Bechtold, Carl. Member of Colorado's winning Jeffers Cup team, 1939.

Bellmar, Fred Cyril. Member of Zipfelberger Club; co-founder of Red Mountain Lodge in 1930s; president of SRMSA, 1941-48; president of Nat. Ski Association, 1948-54; Blegen Plaque, 1950; CSHF.

Benedict, Fritz. 10th Mt. Div.; Aspen instructor; architect in Aspen; designed Snowmass; chief organizer of 10th Mt. Trail Association for hut system in Aspen area. CSHF.

Berge, Trgve. Director of original ski school, Breckenridge. CSHF.

Berger, George, Jr. Early Arlberg member; an initial investor with Colorado National Bank in Aspen; first president of Aspen Ski Corporation.

Berger, Miriam. Early member of Arlberg Club.

Bergman, William. Iowa lawyer who promoted financing for Keystone resort.

Berry, Ray and Josephine. Developed Monarch Ski Area from T-bar through chairlift.

Billings, Norton. U.S. Olympic team, 1932. CSHF

Blickensderfer, J. C. Pioneer Denver skier in Arlberg and Zipfelberger Clubs; helped build early tows and bridges, and Trap Door lodge; co-owner of original Denver ski shop.

Boehm, Karl. 10th Mt. Div.; founded Peaceful Valley ski touring center.

Boettcher, Charles. Pioneer in Denver skiing; helped plan original Trap Door Lodge.

Bookstrom, Hans M. Active coach for Junior Ski Club Zipfelberger; National Ski Jumping Judge. CSHF.

Borkovec, Steve. WSC skier; X-C champion; director of ski touring at Crested Butte.

Bowles, James A. Breckenridge manager who built alpine slide.

Boyce, Kelly. Founder of Wolf Creek Pass ski area.

Boyce, Paul. Member of Breckenridge team which won international speed record, 1983.

Bradley, Steve. Made noted trek from Ashcroft to Crested Butte in 1930s; CU coach;manager, Winter Park; supervised Balcony House Lodge; laid out original Mary Jane runs; inventor of Bradley Packer Grader and known as "Father of Slope Maintenance;" president of Nat. Ski Areas Association; helped organize CSC-USA; Burton Trophy, 1938; Layman Trophy; Halstead Award; CSHF.

Branch, Tom. Worked at least 36 years with youth in Eskimo Ski Club, Denver and Winter Park. Eskimos have introduced 50,000 children to skiing. CSHF

Braun, Alfred E. Manager of ski hut system in Elk Mountains.

Bray, Andy. Crested Butte pioneer jumper who leaped over railroad trains in 1800s.

Briner, Gordon. Director of Arapahoe Basin and Keystone ski schools.

Briner, John. "Dean of Colorado Ski School Directors;" original, longtime director of Purgatory school.

Brookshank, Scott. Nat. exhibition skiing champion, Vail, 1972.

Brown, D. R. C. "Darcy." Charter member of Denver's Zipfelberger Club; original investor and planner, Aspen; president of Aspen Ski Corporation; president of Colorado Passenger Tramway Safety Board; helped found CSC-USA; CSHF.

Brown, Frank. Nat. jr. champion; CU NCAA All American, 1950 Olympian, 1964.

Buchtel, Henry. Early Denver CMC skier; opposed Telemark style.

Bulkley, Frank. Helped found Trap Door Lodge; founded early ski supply business in Denver; founded Eskimo Ski Club; established first ski rental system in Denver; CSHF.

Burritt, John. WSC skier; Olympian, biathlon, 1960; established Grand Mesa ski touring trail system.

Button, Horace. Pioneer Hot Sulphur Springs skier and companion of Carl Howelson; developed ski program and facilities at Hot Sulphur Springs; CSHF.

Butts, Dave. CU NCAA jumping champion, 1959; downhill, 1960; Skimeister Award,1959.

Calloway, Howard "Bo". Investor who revived Crested Butte.

Chaffee, Rick. DU NCAA slalom-alpine combined champion, 1965; Nat. men's giant slalom champion, 1968.

Chase, Curt. 10th Mt. Div.; directed Aspen and Snowmass ski schools. CSHF.

Christensen, Peik. DU NCAA slalom champion, 1973, 1974; Alpine combined in 1974.

Clayton, Dr. Mack L. Specialist in winter sports injuries; a founder of Mt. Werner area; founder of U.S. Ski Team Physicians; CSHF.

Comstam, E. G. Inventor of T-bar lift; installed longest in world at that time at Camp Hale.

Coors, Adolph III. Instrumental in bringing World Alpine Ski Campionships to Aspen in 1950--first time event held in U.S. CSHF.

Cornwall, Harry C. Pioneer at Irwin whose account of skiing there in the 1880s is one of the earliest descriptions of races and clubs in the nation.

Cotton, Ken. Original manager of Breckenridge.

Couch, Edmund. DU early skier; ski jump engineer for more than 150 sites; certified nat. jumping judge; skied with Prestrud at Dillon; CSHF; NSHF.

Cranmer, George. Denver Parks and Recreation manager who founded Winter Park; CSHF.

Crawford, Gary. Steamboat Springs Olympian, 1980.

Crawford, Marvin. Steamboat Springs and DU; Nat. Jr. Champion, 1946; 1948, 1950; NCAA X-C and Skimeister, 1954; FIS, 1954; Olympian, 1956; first manager Storm Mountain (Mount Werner); CSHF; Colorado Sports Hall of Fame

Cress, Jennings. DU NCAA, 1964 Skimeister.

Cress, John. DU NCAA, 1956 Skimeister, 1960 Nordic Olympian.

Cullman, Duncan. Breckenridge speed skiing team, 1983 international champions.

Cunningham, Gerry. 10th Mt. Div.; founded Gerry's Mountain Sports business.

Dahle, Gunnar. Pioneer skier at Parshall and Steamboat Springs.

d'Albazi, Lt. One of Denver's earliest ski instructors, from Italian army.

Dalpes, James Louis. Colorado's first all-American team member; 1931; Steamboat Springs skijoring champion; manager, Winter Park; CSHF.

Darley, George M. Skiing Presbyterian minister who preached at mining camps in 1800s.

Davis, Wilfred "Slim." USFS ranger who helped found several ski areas, including Glenwood Springs' Red Mountain; CSHF.

Demers, Eddie. WSC NCAA 1963; 1964 X-C champion; Nat. men's X-C champion, 1964; FIS, 1962; Olympian, 1964.

Dendahl, John. CU NCAA X-C, Nordic champion, 1960; Skimeister, 1960; Olympian X-C, 1960, 1964. de Pret, Count Phillipe. Belgian ski instructor, Broadmoor, 1930s.

Dercum, Edna. Pennsylvania state women's downhill and slalom champion, 1941; with husband, Max, founded Ski Tip Lodge; helped found Arapahoe and Keystone, Nat. Veteran skier women's champion, 1967 and 1970; author of It's Easy, Edna, It's Downhill All the Way; CSHF.

Dercum, Max. Cornell University skier, coach and forestry professor; founded Ski Tip Lodge; original investor and cofounder of Arapahoe and Keystone; helped originate Professional Ski Instructors of America, 1961; won world giant slalom championship for over 60; Nat. Vet's champion, 1970; first inductee of **Ski** magazine Hall of Fame; CSHF; NSHF.

Dercum, Rolf. Outstanding jr. and DU skier.

Devecka, Mike. Only U.S. skier to win national championships in all three Nordic disciplines; U.S. Olympic team. All-American at Fort Lewis College, D.U. coach. CSHF.

Dole, Minot "Minnie." Founder and first president of Nat. Ski Patrol; originator of idea for ski troops and 10th Mt. Div.; author of Adventures in Skiing; CSHF; NSHF.

Duke, H. Benjamin Jr. 10th Mt. Division Historian, leader of Division Resource Center; activve in Vail Development. CSHF.

Duncan, J. J. Nat. downhill champion, 1934 for Estes Park Ski Club.

Duncan, Ray. Original investor and promoter of Purgatory.

Durrance, Dick. America's most famous skier of 1930s; Olympic coach, 1936; first Harriman Cup winner, 1937; Nat. champion, 1937-41; made noted Ashcroft Crested Butte pioneer X-C trek, 1930s; SRMSA champion, 1941; mountain manager and general manager, Aspen; brought FIS to Aspen, 1950; original investor and cofounder of Arapahoe; American Ski Trophy; Halstead Memorial Trophy; CSHF; NSHF.

Dwyer, Charles "Chuck." Veteran ski lift engineer; Chief Aerial Tramway Engineer, USFS; author of Aerial Tramways, Ski Lifts, and Tows: Description and Terminology.

Dyer, John. Pioneer Methodist clergyman and mail carrier in Fairplay area, early 1860s; author of The Snowshoe Itinerant; CSHF.

Eaton, Earl V. Prospector who discovered Vail as ski area.

Eaton, Margaret. Leader in promotion of U.S. ski teams and racing clubs. CSHF

Eflin, Dick. An original investor and developer at Crested Butte.

Elisha, Laurence. One of the original developers of Aspen Mountain; owned Hotel Jerome.

Elisha, M. J. CU coach, 1966-67.

Ellefsen, Didrik. CU NCAA jumping champion, 1974; Schoenberger Award.

Elliot, Jere. Steamboat Springs Olympian, 1960, 1968.

Elliot, Jon. Steamboat Springs Olympian, 1960, 1968.

Elliott, Mike. Fort Lewis College and CU; 1960 nat. jr. champion; 1966 nat. X-C champion; Finlandia Trophy, 1964, 1965, and 1971; Burton Trophy, 1971, 1972; nat. Nordic champion, 1970, 1971, 1972; manager, planning and development, Purgatory. CSHF.

Engel, Ernst. Cornell University coach; 10th Mt. Div.; noted ski wear designer.

Engel, George. Director of Winter Park Ski School, 1946-82. CSHF.

Engren, Karle. Member of 1939 Colorado champion Jeffers Cup team.

Eriksen, Stein. Norwegian champion who moved to Aspen; among top ten all-time world champion racers; 1954 Olympic gold medal; FIS champion, 1950, 1954; Holmenkollen-Kandahar slalom champion, 1949, 1954; Harriman Cup, 1953; Lauberhorn slalom champion, 1951, 1952; pioneered inverted aerials; author of Come Ski with Me; Aspen and Aspen Highlands ski school instructor; director of skiing at Deer Valley, Park City, Utah, and owner of lodge there; NSHF.

Esmiol, Merritt. USFS snow ranger and skiing historian.

Evans, Roger. Crested Butte nat. freestyle champion.

Fairfield-Smith, H. Breckenridge international championship speed skiing team member, 1983.

Farwell, Ted. DU NCAA Nordic and all-American, 1959. CSHF.

Ferguson, Ian. Publicist, veteran Zipfelburger; Halstead Award. CSHF.

Ferno, Mike. Salida mayor who led development of Monarch, 1939.

Ferries-Arroyo, Barbara. Nat. jr. Champion, 1960; CU team; Harriman Cup, 1961; FIS (third) 1962; Vail Cup, 1963; Olympic Bronze Medal, 1964; NSHF.

Fetcher, John. Steamboat Springs rancher, a founder of Storm Mountain; led drive to refurbish Howelsen Hill; CSHF.

Fiske, Billy. Olympic bobsled team, 1928, 1932 gold medal winner; founded Highland Bavarian Corporation to develop Ashcroft, 1936-37; killed in action as RAF volunteer, World War II.

Flood, Eyvind. Pioneer skier at Montezuma and Dillon areas.

Floystad, Oyvind. DU NCAA jumping champion; 1962.

Flynn, Tom J. Aspen area skier who helped found Highland Bavarian Lodge at Ashcroft, 1936-37.

Ford, Grant. National referee; veteran Zipfelberger; Halstead Award; CSHF

Ford, Mark. CU NCAA downhill, combined champion, 1975; Schoenberger Award, 1975.

Foster, Bill. Active promoter, developer, Powderhorn.

Fowler, Donald S. United Airlines executive who promoted ski industry in Colorado; CSHF.

Frame, Bill and Mary. Founded ski touring center at ghost town of Elkton near Crested Butte.

Froelicher, Charles. Headmaster of Colorado Academy who was a founder of Copper Mountain.

Gallagher, Mike. CU skier who won 13 X-C titles, more than any other US Nordic competitor; Nat. Men's X-C champion many years, 1962 on; FIS, 1964-76; Olympian, 1964, 1968, 1972, 1976; US Nordic coach, 1971; US X-C Olympic coach, 1980; Burton Trophy, 1966, 1967, 1970; Finlandia Trophy, 1966, 1977.

Gansen, Ole-Ivar. DU NCAA X-C champion, 1970, 1971.

Gardiner, Charles Fox. 1800s skiing doctor who wrote <u>Doctor at Timberline</u>.

Garland, Earl. Helped found Red Mountain ski area at Glenwood Springs.

Geier, Hans. President of Steamboat Springs Ski Area.

Gibbons, James. Skiing priest of San Juans, 1800s; author of <u>In the San Juan, Colorado: Sketches</u>.

Gorsuch, Dave. Nat. jr. Champion, 1956; FIS, 1958; Olympian, 1960; Nat. down hill champion, 1962; WSC NCAA downhill champion, 1963; Nat. Veterans' champion, 1970; manager of Crested Butte; operates ski shops at Vail; White Stag Trophy, 1962. CSHF.

Gorsuch, George. Early USFS snow ranger.

Gorsuch, Jack. Operator of Climax in 1950s.

Gramshammer, Pepi. Austrian ski champion with six international pro championships, inlcuding 1951 Tirol; Vail instructor. CSHF.

Grant, Bill. Early Denver Arlberg Club; developed Berthoud area, 1948.

Grant, Edwin H. Successfully promoted Groswald skis for 10th Mountain Division. CSHF.

Grant, Neil. Early member of Denver Arlberg Club.

Gray, Bob. CU X-C champion; won 15 km in 1961; US Nordic titles 1971-73; FIS 1962, 1966, 1970; Olympian 1968, 1972; Finlandia Trophy, 1970.

Grazier, Mike. Freestyle champion from Crested Butte.

Groswold, Gerald. Original investory in Storm Mountain; president of Winter Park; with Harald Sorenson, directed US youth jumping program. CSHF.

Groswold, Thor. CSHF.

Hackney, Edgar. New York original investor, Aspen.

Haemerle, Florian. European champion who taught at Berthoud in 1930s; charter member of Zipfelberger Club.

Hall, Henry. Michigan skier; Nat. jumping champion at Steamboat Springs, 1917; NSHF.

Hammernes, Odd. DU NCAA jumping champion, 1969, 1972.

Hannah, Joan. Olympian; Vail instructor.

Hansen, Hans. Very early competitor at Steamboat Springs; Genesee Mountain, 1920.

Hansen, Ole-Jval. DU NCAA x-country champion 1970-1971.

Harsh, James L. Pioneer skier at Hot Sulphur Springs; 1917 Winter Carnival there; founded ski club at Colorado A & M, 1932; Olympian alternate, 1932; re-activated Estes Park Ski Club, 1946; CSHF.

Haugen, Anders. Famed ski jumper, originally from South Dakota, who made records at Hot Sulphur Springs, Dillon and Steamboat Springs; Nat. champion jumper, 1920, 1926; Captain of first US Winter Olympic team, 1924; first winner of medal in winter Olympics for US; later instructor at Lake Tahoe, California; CSHF; NSHF.

Haugen, Lars. Brother of Anders who won six nat. jumping championships between 1912 and 1928; pioneer jumper at Hot Sulphur Springs, Dillon and Steamboat Springs; later instructor at Lake Tahoe, California; CSHF; NSHF.

Hauk, Paul. Early member and competitive skier for Colorado A & M Ski Club; participant in Colorado's first intercollegiate meet at Berthoud Pass; USFS snow ranger; inventoried Colorado ski terrain; influenced construction of many resort areas; official USFS surveyor; avalanche patrol for Squaw Valley Olympics, 1960; historian of White River National Forest ski areas; CSHF.

Hayes, George P. Major General, commander, 10th Mt. Div.

Head, Howard. Founder of Sports Medicine Center at Vail; Inventor of Head Skis. CSHF.

Heron, Robert and Kenneth "Webb." Founders of Heron Construction, pioneer builders of Colorado lifts. CSHF.

Heuga, Jim. Aspen nat. jr. Champion, 1960; White Band slalom winner, 1960, Roch Cup, 1962; CU NCAA slalom champion, 1963; Arlberg Kandahar, 1964; Harriman Cup, 1962; Olympic bronze medal winner, 1964; NSHF Athlete of the

Year Award, 1964; Beck International Trophy, 1967; Wallace Werner Award, 1967; US Ski Writers' Outstanding Competitor Award, 1967; NSHF; technical director of Lange Company; Director of Racing for Beconta, Inc., Lake Tahoe, California.   CSHF.

Higgs, John. Chicago developer of Sunlight.

Hilton, Conrad. Hotel magnate who was original Aspen investor.

Hinderman, Tim. CU winner of 1971 Schoenberger Award; CU coach beginning 1979.

Hinkley, Don. Durnago skier who won 1972 Gelande races.

Hitchcock, Peter. Crested Butte skier who won 1976 Gelande races.

Hlavata, Jana. Nordic Olympian, 1972, 1976; X-C director at Keystone.

Hodges, Bill and Joe. Early Arlberg Club members; original Aspen investors.   CSHF.

Hoeschler, Jim. Student CU coach, 1967-69.

Holden, John. Founder of Colorado Rocky Mountain School who established ski hut system in Elk Mountains.

Holmen-Jensen, Tom. CU NCAA jumping champion, 1978; Schoenberger Award, 1978.

Horiuche, Harold. Zipfelberger; veteran partrolman and timer; wrote Manual Timing, definitive guide for U.S. races. CSHF.

Hosberg, Jim. Co-founder of Red Mountain Lodge.

Howard, Menefree R. Original leader of CMC Denver Winter Sports Club; pur chased land for Genesee Mountain.

Howelsen, Carl. Father of competitive and recreational skiing in Colorado; winner of Holmenkollen; introduced sport skiing at Hot Sulphur Springs, Steamboat Springs and Genesee Mountain; Nat. jumper, 1921; CSHF; NSHF.

Huddleston, Sam. Denver landscape architect who helped found Storm Mountain area at Steamboat Springs.

Hudspeth, Jim. Member of Colorado team which won Jeffers Cup, 1939.

Hughes, Berrian. First Colorado skiing fatality except for avalanche, Loveland Pass, Hughes Run at Winter Park named in his memory.

Huntington, Sam. Member of Colorado Jeffers Cup Team, 1939; developer and manager of Berthoud, 1948.

Iselin, Fred. Famed Sun Valley skier who moved to Aspen as instructor; Aspen Highlands; author of Invitation to Skiing; CSHF; NSHF.

Jacobs, Tom. CU coach, 1951-55; secretary of Nat. Ski Association.

Jankovsky, Joe. Manager of Arapahoe Basin; headed group which bought it in 1972.

Janss, William. Stanford University skier and 1940 Olympian; early developer of Snowmass.

Jansen, Erik. DU NCAA jumping champion, 1964, 1965; Nordic, 1964.

Jay, John. 10th Mt. Div. Official photographer; Aspen photographer and film producer for American skiing.

Jencks, Moses Amos. Professor who started first collegiate ski program in West, WSC, 1916.

Johnson, Albert. "Snowshoe Expressman" who carried mail from Crystal to Crested Butte in 1880s; CSHF.

Johnstone, Robert C. Zipfelberger; active in Winter Park development and Colorado college and university programs. Halstead Award. CSHF

Jones, Greg. CU winner, US Alpine Competitor of the Year, 1975; won three FIS races in seven days, a new feat for an American skier.

Jones, Mark. Won Gelande, Vail, 1972.

Jones, "Whip." Developer of Aspen Highlands; original promoter of Breckenridge; investor at Vail and Sunlight.

Judd, William R. Founded first Colorado ski patrol at Hidden Valley, 1938; founded Seven Sentinels mountain rescue team, forerunner of rescue groups; Nat. Ski Patrol; CSHF.

Juhan, Joe. Leased Glenwood's Red Mountain in 1950s.

Jump, Larry. Dartmouth skier captured in World War II, released; 10th Mt. Div.; Founded Arapahoe Basin; a founder of Rocky Mountain Ski Operations Association; pioneered handicapped and first amputee programs; promoter and dealer of Poma lifts; CSHF.

Jump, Marnie. Cited for work in developing programs for handicapped skiers.

Kane, Jim. Early leader of Salida Winter Sports Club.

Kashiwa, Hank. President of Boulder ski manufacturing company; CBS TV ski broadcast commentator. CSHF

Kendall, Bob. CU winner of US Nordic combined, FIS, 1970; Olympian, 1972.

Kendrick, Charles. Member of original tournament committee for SRMSA.

Kendrick, Jack. Pioneer Denver enthusiast; chairman of winter sports for Denver; instrumental in founding Winter Park.

Kidd, William "Billy." CU champion; Olympic silver medal, 1964; FIS gold medal, Alpine combined, 1970; Val Gardena (Italy) silver medal, 1970; World Cup, 1970; US Ski Writers' Outstanding Competitor Award, 1970; Pro Skier of the Year, 1970; NSHF Athlete of the Year, 1964 and 1970; Steamboat Springs Director of Skiing; fostered Kidd Cowboy Race; with Sven Wiik, founded first International Special Olympics, 1976; director of Billy Kidd Racing Camps. CSHF.

Kidder, Arthur W. Outstanding national amputee skier; Nat. Ski Patrol Leader, CSHF.

Kidder-Lee, Barbara. Nation's premier skier, 1946; Roch Cup, 1946, NSHF. CSHF.

Kinney, Mark. Champion ski jumper from Steamboat Springs.

Klumb, Larry. Early manager at Powderhorn.

Knowlton, Steve. University of New Hampshire team; 10th Mt. Div.; Olympian, 1948; founded Golden Horn restaurant, Aspen; developed, coached Aspen junior skiing program; nat. champion, 1946; manager of Ski Broadmoor; executive director of RMSA; first executive director, CSC-USA; founder of Kandahar Restaurant and Ski Museum, Littleton; CSHF; NSHF.

Koch, Bill. Durango Olympian Nordic, 1976 silver medal, 1984.

Krog, George. DU NCAA champion, Nordic combined, 1969.

Kuss, Adolph. WSC champion; Fort Lewis College coach; 1964 Olympic X-C coach. CSHF.

Lafferty, Mike. CU NCAA champion, downhill, 1966, 1969; best international downhill record in US history; Olympian, 1972.

Lake, Rial. Developer, Gunnison Ski Club, 1930s; a founder of Pioneer ski area, first chairlift in state.

La Munyan, Ed. Outstanding junior skier at Steamboat Springs, 1920s.

Lang, Otto. Designer of skis for Groswold plant in Denver; nationally-famed skier.

Lange, Robert B. Inventor of injection-molded plastic ski boot and new ski design. Helped found Pro Racing Tour. CSHF

Larkin, James R. "Gus." Longtime manager of Crested Butte.

Larsh, Don. WSC champion; director of first Cooper Hill ski school.

Lawrence, Andrea Mead. From Vermont, and later Parshall, Colorado; listed among best all-time women skiers; FIS 1950; Nat. women's slalom and giant slalom champion, 1949 and 1953; Olympic winner, giant slalom and slalom, 1952; first American skier to win two gold medals; Harriman Cup, 1950, 1953; Nat. women's slalom and Alpine combined champion, 1955; Beck International Trophy, 1952; White Stag Trophy, 1955; NSHF; first skier nominee to US Olympic Hall of Fame,1983.

Lawrence, Dave. Nat. ski champion; FIS 1950, Aspen; NSHF; coach, women's Olympic team.

Letson, Ed. WSC Olympian, 1960.

Levy, Lynn. WSC Olympian, 1960.

Lewis, Charles D. "Chuck." Vice president, Vail; later principal founder and manager, Copper Mountain.

Litchfield, Johnny. 10th Mt. Div.; Aspen ski instructor; founder of Red Onion Restaurant, Aspen.

Little, Rogers. CU NCAA All-American, 1969; US Men's Alpine team, 1971, 1972.

Livingston, Lou. Developer of National Ski First Aid; operator of Estes Park youth hostel. CSHF

Lodders, Georgia. Long time Area Operations Director, CSC-USA   CSHF.

L'Orange, John. DU NCAA slalom champion, 1954 (first NCAA meet).

Lynch, Kerry. Grand Lake and WSC; US Nordic champion, 1981; won Holmenkollen King's Cup; Olympian, 1984.

Mac Lennan, Kenneth. WSC coach since 1969.

Mace, Stewart. Operated dog-sled and X-C resort, Ashcroft.

Madigan, Mike. Denver Post writer who won Hirsch Award for most effective ski writing, 1975.

Magnifico, Mike. Aspen skier who helped lay out original Ajax Mountain site; active in later development; Aspen mountain trail named in his honor.

Mahoney, Billy. First manager of Telluride.   CSHF.

Malin, Jeff. Crested Butte skier who compiled best individual records, International Speed Skiing Association, 1983.

Marolt, Bill. Aspen jr. nat. champion, 1959, 1960; CU NCAA downhill champion, 1963, 1965; US nat. champion, 1963, 1965; Olympian, 1964; CU athletic director, 1969-78; Schoenberger Award, 1966; Alpine director, US Ski Team, 1980; US Olympic coach.   CSHF.

Marolt, Bud. Nat. jr. champion, 1950, from Aspen.

Marshall, Jack. President and chief executive officer, Vail.

Martin, Todd. Second executive director, CSC-USA.

Martin-Kuntz, Marti. Telluride instructor; world champion speed skier in women's classification.

Masbruch, Evelyn. First woman on U.S. Ski Assn. board of directors; fund raiser for U.S. National and Olympic teams. CSHF.

Matis, Clark. US Army X-C team; CU NCAA X-C champion, 1968, 1969; Nat. men's X-C champion, 15 km, 30 km, 1969, 1970; Schoenberger Award, 1969.

Matt, Toni. New York and Oregon winner, 1941 SRMSA; 10th Mt. Div.; nat. champion, 1939, 1940; U.S. combined champion, 1941; Harriman Cup, 1939; FIS, 1950; NSHF.

Maynard, Robert. President and chief executive officer for Ralston-Purina's Keystone and Arapahoe ski areas; former Assistant Director, National Park Service. CSHF.

McCoy, Dennis. DU NCAA champion, 1967, 1968.

McDermott, Wes. Leader in Gunnison Ski Club, 1930s, who helped establish Pioneer ski area.

McDonald, Otto. Nineteenth-century skiing mail carrier in Crested Butte area.

McGill, Tim. Steamboat Springs nat. Gelande champion, 1983.

McGowan, Graeme. Founder of Arlberg Club, Denver; helped establish West Portal trails; conducted first organized races for CMC, 1929, 1930; ski instructor, U. S. Army Engineers, World War II; developed lodge and ski instruction at Purgatory.

McGrane, Dennis. Littleton Olympian, jumping, 1984.

McKinney, Steve. Speed skiing champion, 1974 and 1978; 124.34 miles per hour at Silverton meet.

McLean, Robert "Barney". Pioneer skier of Hot Sulphur Springs; charter member of Zipfelberger Club; member of Colorado Jeffers Cup championship team, 1939; Olympian jumper, 1936; captain, Olympic jumping, racing, 1948; first winner of Roch Cup, 1946; Harriman Cup, 1942; U. S. nat. champion, 1942; FIS, 1950; designer of skis for Groswold plant, Denver; CSHF; NSHF; Colorado Sports Hall of Fame.

McMurtry, John. U.S. Olympic skier; Author of <u>United States Ski Team Alpine Skiing Manual</u> in 1976. CSHF

McReady, John. Denver banker who bailed out faltering Storm Mountain development at Steamboat Springs.

Merrill, Hollis. Steamboat Springs jr. skier; taught by Howelsen.

Merrill, Marcellus. Pioneer Steamboat Springs skier; jumped with Howelsen and Prestrud; partner with Thor Groswold in ski manufacturing, Denver; inventor of a metal ski, three-point binding; a cartop carrier, roller devices for Steamboat skiing band; established Merrill Trophy in 1940 for Steamboat Springs Winter Carnival; CSHF.

Meyers, Charlie. Denver Post and **Ski** magazine writer who won Hirsch Award for most effective ski writing, 1977. CSHF.

Mill, Andy. Aspen U. S. Alpine champion, 1975; World Cup racer. U.S. Olympic team; National downhill champion; 1976. TV network commentator. CSHF.

Mills, Enos. Founder of Ski Idlewild. CSHF.

Miller, Dwight. Founder of Ski Idlewild.

Miller, Earnest. Original ski classification member, SRMSA.

Miller, Jim. Fort Lewis College NCAA champion, Nordic, 1968; nat. Nordic champion, 1969, 1970; NSHF Athlete of the Year, 1970.

Miller, Mack. Nat. jr. champion, 1949; WSC NCAA X-C champion, 1957; Olympian, Nordic champion, 1957; Olympian, Nordic, 1956, 1960; FIS, 1958; Burton Trophy, 1956.

Miller, Warren. Premier producer of ski movies. CSHF.

Mills, Enos C. Naturalist whose efforts established Rocky Mountain National Park; pioneer in skiing for scientific research.

Milstein, Richard. Founder of Conquistador.

Mitchell, R. Garrett. Vice President at Copper Mountain; executive director of Colorado Ski Country USA, 1976.

Mize, Dick. WSC team and Olympian biathlon team, 1960.

Molterer, Anderl. Austrian instructor at Aspen; won Hohnenkamm Races, 1953, 1955, 1958, 1959; Arlberg Kandahar, 1953, 1954; Lauberhorn, 1953, 1956, 1957; Grand Prix du Megeve, 1959.

Monson, D. Steamboat Springs nat. Nordic winner, Estes Park, 1934.

Morris, John. Aspen and Colorado Springs skier; first director of Sunlight ski school.

Moulton, William "Bill." Development director for Mamn's Peak, near Rifle.

Murri, Robert. Manager, Loveland Basin; helped found Colorado Ski Country USA.

Neusteter, Myron. Active Denver skier in 1930s who helped promote idea of mountain resorts.

Nevins, Hugh J. Air support officer for 10th Mountain Division; World's most decorated combat glider pilot in World War II. CSHF

Nielson, Don. Boulder Olympian, biathlon, 1984.

Nilsen, Egil. CU NCAA champion, X-C, 1982; Schoenberger Award, 1982.

Nilsgard, Vidar. CU NCAA jumping champion, 1971, 1973; Schoenberger Award, 1973.

Nilson, Swan. Nineteenth-century skiing mail carrier killed in San Juan snowslide, 1883.

Nitze, Paul. Initial investor in Aspen; later majority stockholder; among initial investors, Snowmass; U. S. Secretary of Navy; later U. S. Arms Reduction negotiator.

Obermeyer, Klaus. Founder of a Denver manufacturing company for his invention of the double boot. CSHF.

O'Leary, Hal. Pioneer in amputee skiing programs; author of Bold Tracks: Skiing for the Disabled. CSHF.

Olson, Willis "Billy." DU NCAA jumping champion, 1954, 1955, 1956; FIS 1950, 1954; Olympian 1952, 1956; NSHF.

Omtvedt, Ragner. Canadian who made world record jump at Steamboat Springs, 1917; U. S. nat. champion, 1913, 1914, 1917; NSHF.

Opaas, Kjetil. CU champion jumper; Schoenberger Award, 1980.

Ormes, Robert M. Colorado Springs guidebook author who has collected old ski songs.

Overland, Terje. DU NCAA champion, 1966, 1967; later pro skier.

Paepcke, Elizabeth. "Discovered" Aspen and introduced her husband, Walter, to its charms.

Paepcke, Walter. President of Container Corporation of America who dedicated himself to development of Aspen as a skiing and cultural center, founding Aspen Ski Corporation; CSHF.

Panion, Paul. Engineer of original lift at Crested Butte.

Parent, Alec. Skiing mail carrier at Tin Cup, 1880s, making runs over Tin Cup and Cumberland passes.

Parker, Robert W. Mount Rainier guide who later served in 10th Mt. Div.; New York state team; St. Lawrence University team; Pacific downhill champion; leader in Aspen development; set up Aspen's first pro ski patrol; original public relations director, Vail; editor of Ski magazine; president, Vail Associates; shepherded Beaver Creek development; helped create Colorado Ski Country USA; instrumental in creation of Colorado Ski Museum and Hall of Fame, Vail; Senior Vice President for Operations at Vail after 1980; Golden Quill award, 1975; CSHF.

Patterson, William A. Initial investor at Aspen.

Pearson, Dale. CU Schoenberger Award, 1979.

Pedersen, Olav. Breckenridge; "Father of Ski for Light in U. S.," a racing program for the blind.

Peet, Barney. Fort Lewis NCAA downhill champion, 1968.

Perchlick, Dick. Founded Sharktooth, 1971.

Perry, Henry. Denver banker who helped bail out faltering Storm Mountain at Steamboat Springs.

Perry, Marjorie. Pioneer woman skier of Steamboat Springs; persuaded Carl Howelsen to move to Steamboat.   CSHF.

Perry, Robert. Member of Colorado's Jeffers Cup winners, 1939; prominent Aspen skier after World War II; president of Sunlight, 1969.

Perry-Smith, Crosby. 10th Mt. Div. And WSC champion; Olympian, 1952; FIS 1950, 1954; Winter Park instructor; Steamboat Springs jr. champion.

Pesman, Jerry. Grand Junction, first National Veterans' Champion, 1960; helped plan Montezuma Basin; later Boulder resident, founder, with Joe Jonas, of Master Ski Series.   CSHF.

Peterson, Dick. President, Vail Associates; later headed Purgatory.

Pew, Bill. Steamboat Springs man who ski-treked 450 miles along Continental Divide to publicize bill for trail development.

Pfeifer, Freidl. Famed European skier who instructed at Sun Valley; later 10th Mt. Div.; nat. champion, 1940; Harriman Cup, 1939, 1940; Silver Belt award, 1940; original developer of Aspen following World War II, with Paepcke; developed Buttermilk; CSHF.

Phelps, Ken. WSC Olympian, 1968.

Phipps, Allan. Promoter of Winter Park development. CSHF.

Pitcher, Bill K. Aspen instructor who did preliminary work there; later owned Santa Fe Basin; consultant to Big Sky in Montana.

Porcarelli, Mike. CU NCAA slaloms, combined champion, 1970, 1972; Schoenberger Award, 1970, 1972.

Praeger, Walter. Dartmouth coach, instructor 10th Mt. Div.; Olympic coach, Alpine, 1948; Winter Park instructor; NSHF.

Prendergast, James. Instructor, manager, Crested Butte area; later on Sunlight staff.

Prestrud, Peter. Pioneer jumper at Dillon and Steamboat Springs; led construction of original Dillon jump; CSHF.

Pyles, Rudd. FIS, 1970; Olympian, 1972; outstanding professional skier; pro director for Spaulding, 1976.

Pyles, Scott. WSC International Intercollegiate downhill champion, 1968; Roch Cup, 1970; professional skier, 1971.

Pytte, Peder. DU coach, 1970-1975; DU NCAA all-American, 1956.   CSHF.

Rachetto, Paul. DU NCAA slalom and combined champion, 1969.

Rahm, John. Denver pioneer skier who helped develop West Portal, 1936; manager, Breckenridge, 1970-1977.

Ralston, Norman. Colorado's earliest competitive jr. skier; jumped in Genesee meet at age of seven, 1920.

Rand, Jay. Nat. jr. champion, jumping, 1966; CU NCAA champion, 1970; Olympian, 1968.

Reilly, Barney. Outstanding early Denver skier who represented that city in original Genesee meet, 1920.

Reischl, Steve. WSC FIS, 1962; NCAA jumping champion, 1962; Bietila Trophy, 1962. CSHF.

Richardson, Tom. President and Chief Executive Officer, Aspen, after its acquisition by Twentieth Century Fox, 1979.

Rideout, Perry. Former Dartmouth skier, 10th Mt. Div.; an original instructor at post–World War II Aspen.

Riiber, Harold. DU NCAA Nordic combined champion, 1959; all-American, 1959.

Roberts, Curtis William. Lakewood skitouring champion in Medals for Miles program, 1977; made top mileage of 2,020 in one season.

Robinson, Vernon "V.J." Mainstay in survival of early Denver ski clubs; brought national championship tournament to Colorado in 1921. CSHF

Roch, Andre. European expert who laid out original trails on Ajax Mountain, Aspen; Roch's Run, Roch Cup named for him.

Rockefeller, J. R. Nineteenth Century skiing doctor, Gunnison.

Rodolph, Katy. Outstanding Steamboat Springs jr. skier; nat. women's downhill CSHF.

Rogers, James Grafton. A founder of Colorado Mountain Club, which spawned several ski clubs.

Rolfe, Colonel Onslow S. "Pinkie." Commander, 10th Mt. Div.

Romine, Mike. Student CU coach, 1967-1969; nat. X-C team, 1966-1972.

Ronnestad, Oddvar. DU NCAA jumping, all-American Alpine, 1958.

Rounds, Bill. Founder of Breckenridge.

Rowen, Robert. Original investor, Highland Bavarian Lodge, Ashcroft, 1937.

Rowland, Harold "Red." Engineer of lifts at Aspen, Buttermilk, Snowmass, Breckenridge; general manager, later vice-president, engineering, Aspen, Red Rover and Rover's Run at Buttermilk named for him; CSHF. champion, 1951, 1953; White Stag Trophy, 1953; Steamboat Springs instructor; CU champion; CSHF.

Runette, Evelyn. Original and longtime general secretary of SRMSA; executive secretary of Rocky Mountain Ski Association, 1940-1951; CSHF.

Russell, Bob. USFS ranger who promoted first "National Ski Trail" designation for Crag Crest on Grand Mesa.

Ryan, Ted. Original investor and co-founder, Highland Bavarian Lodge, Ashcroft, 1937. CSHF.

Sabich, Vladimir "Spider." CU champion, winner of the Schoenberger award, 1967; U.S. Alpine and downhill champion, 1969. NSHF Athlete of the year, 1970; two time pro champion, greatest pro moneymaker in 1971 winning $50,650, K-2 pro team, 1973; accidentally shot to death at age thirty-one, 1976.

Sabin, Mary S. A founder of Colorado Mountain Club.

Sattersum. John. Noted skier who rode out a massive snowslide on Schofield Pass in 1880s.

Sayre. J. E. Donated land for Glenwood Springs' original Red Mountain Dev.

Sayer, Robert. 10th Mt. Div.; a founder of Powderhorn.

Schaeffler, Willy. Noted Austrian and Bavarian resistance fighter, World War II. DU coach 1952-7, 1960-70; his teams won fourteen NCAA championships; U.S. Alpine director, 1970; introduced Wedeln instruction technique; director of ski events, Squaw Valley Olympics 1958-60; established Arapahoe Basin ski school; U.S. Alpine team director, 1970 on; FIS official, 1974; U.S. Ski Association Golden Quill, 1973; Blegen Plaque, 1968; Olympic coach, 1972; listed on several "best coach" ratings; director of winter sports, Disney Productions; CSHF; NSHF; Colorado Sports Hall of Fame.

Schauffler, Frederick "Sandy." Ex-Amherst College skier who was a founder and original investor at Arapahoe Basin.

Schmidt, Agnell. Close friend, fellow skier with Carl Howelsen at Hot Sulphur Springs, 1911.

Schnackenberg, Karl. Noted instructor, Mount Werner.

Schnackenberg, Rudolph E. Instructor, West portal, 1939; instructor, 10th Mt. Div. World War II; helped found SRMSA; Manager Howelsen Hill, Steamboat Springs; instructor, Mount Werner; Colorado College coach, 1950–1951, head instructor, Winter Park; American Instructor of the year Award, 1972–3; CSHF.

Schneibs, Otto. Dartmouth coach who taught at Berthoud in 1930s; wrote American Skiing; designed skis for Groswold of Denver.

Schneider, Hannes. Austrian skier who developed Arlberg system in the early 1900s; later taught in New Hampshire and at Camp Hale's 10th Mt. Div.

Schobinger, Charles W. Designer of uniform trail marking signs world-wide. CSHF

Schoenberger, Dick. Dedicated CU ski supporter, furnishing training site at his ranch near Winter Park; died in 1963; his wife Katie established coveted memorial award in his name for outstanding CU performer each year.

Schwietzer, Charles. Leader in Gunnison Ski Club, 1930s; one of the founders of Pioneer area.

Scott, Bob. Charter member Zipfelberger Club; original member SRMSA tournament committee.

Seibert, Peter W. 10th Mt. Div.; injured in action; taught at Aspen original ski patrol there; FIS 1950; Roch Cup, 1947; taught at Loveland Basin, 1950s; founded Vail ski area; first president, Vail Associates; a founder of Rocky Mountain Ski Operators' Association; helped found Colorado Ski Country U S A; president , Nat. Ski Areas Association , 1973-1975; CSHGF

Selback, Chris. DU NCAA jumping champion, 1961.

Servold, Clarence. DU NCAA X-C champion 1958-9; Nordic, all-American , 1958; nat. men's X-C, 1959.

Severson, Sue and daughter. Aurora team who won Equitable Family Challenge, 1983.

Sharp, W. Edward. Developer of Wolf Creek ski area. CSHF

Shick, Ellen. WSC champion X-C, women's division.

Silverstein, Pete. Early member Denver's Arlberg Club.

Simon, Tom. Aspen speed ski record holder, late 1970s.

Small, Allen. Olympian biathlon; established ski tour center at Tamarron and Purgatory.

Smith, Dudley. Early member Denver's Arlberg Club.

Smith, Margaret "Cap". Attempted to re-vitalize Glenwood's Red Mountain in 1965.

Snoble, Jack. Glenwood Springs collector of ski songs; lore.

Sorensen, Harald "Pop". 10th Mt. Div. Instructor; director, Winter Park school led U.S. youth jumping program there; led **Denver Post** jumping school; winner of awards for youth skiing programs, CSHF; NSHF.

Spence, Gale "Spider." Early volunteer coach and leader in youth skiing. CSHF.

Spencer, Alison Owen. WSC skier and women's coach, 1976; Olympian, 1972.

Staub, Roger. Swiss winner of Holmenkollen-Kandahar, 1959; 1960 Olympian gold medal; instructor, Vail, 1964-1969; director, winter sports, Sniggens Hole, Australia for four seasons; killed in hang glider accident, Switzerland, 1974.

Steele, John. Olympian, 1932; Steamboat Springs' first Olympian; Silver Cup, Hot Sulphur Springs, 1924; helped organize DU ski club; lecturer on joys of skiing who inspired many youth; CSHF.

Stevens, Charles P. Early skiing mail carrier, Tin Cup, 1880s.

Stillman, Richard. Leader in avalanche safety; author of definitive <u>Avalanche Handbook.</u> CSHF.

Sudler, Amos. Early Denver enthusiast who helped develop many CMC projects.

Suttle, Mrs. Steamboat Springs midwife in 1800s who was pulled by skiers on toboggan to help deliver babies. Swenson, Henry. Veteran ski touring racer from Grand Junction; U.S. marathon skiing champion; won five United States Ski Association races for over age sixty in 1983-1984 season.

Swenson, Henry. Veteran ski, touring racer from Grand Junction; US marathon champ; won five US ski assn races for over age 60 in 1983-4; others since then.

Tagert, Billy. Active in development of Ajax Mountain, Aspen.

Taylor, Clif. 10th Mountain Division. Skied for DU and WSC. Noted instructor; set up national programs to promote short skis; author of books on short ski method. NSHF; CSHF.

Taylor, Dick. Copper Mountain Nordic coach, author.

Taylor, Edward F. Co-founder, Red Mountain lodge; founded Colorado School of Mines team; World War II assistant director, Air Force Search and Rescue operations; second director, Nat. Ski Patrol; founder of Rocky Mountain intercollegiate skiing; pioneer in avalanche control; first Coloradoan inducted into NSHF; CSHF.

Temple, Jeff. CU Schoenberger Award, 1976.

Temple, Jim. Founder, Storm Mountain (later Mount Werner).

Thomas, Lowell. Victor native, one of nation's foremost commentators and correspondents; author of many books; publicized skiing throughout nation; covered 10th Mt. Div. in Italy, World War II; Golden Quill, 1977; CSHF; NSHF.

Thompkins, Dick. Helped found Zipfelberger Club; first suggested idea of regional ski association (SRMSA); original classification committee, SRMSA; founded The Ski Shop, Denver, late 1930s. CSHF.

Thompson, Josh. WSC Olympian biathlon, 1984.

Torkle, Torger. International champion, 10th Mt. Div.; killed in action; prestigious trophy named for him; NSHF.

Tschudi, Otto. DU NCAA champion in slalom, giant slalom, downhill, Alpine combined, 1970, 1971, 1972; co-organizer, Pro Racers' Association.

Upham, Tom. CU Schoenberger Award, 1965.

Vaille, Agnes. CMC skier and mountaineer killed in climb of Longs Peak, 1925.

Vaille, Lucretia. Coordinator, Rilliet Hill Club, Denver, 1920s.

Valentine, Don. One of original developers of Storm Mountain at Steamboat Springs.

Valkama, Aarne. DU NCAA Nordic champion, 1963.

Vanatta, Lonny. Outstanding Steamboat Springs pro skier.

Vanderhoof, John. Helped develop Red Mountain and Holiday Hill, Glenwood Springs; governor of Colorado, 1973-1974; director of Western Slope's Club Twenty, an important organization for ski industry promotion.

Vincellette, Alf. DU NCAA jumping champion, all-American, 1957.

Wadsworth, Stan. Leading construction expert at Purgatory.

Waldrop, A. Gayle. Prominent leader in early Boulder Ski Club.

Walker, Gladys. See Werner, Gladys "Skeeter."

Walton, Ralph. Manager, Crested Butte.

Wegeman, Al "Bird." Developed Boy Scout skiing program at Denver, 1930s; first Colorado public school ski coach, Steamboat Springs; first instructor, Winter Park; later Sun Valley instructor; CSHF.

Wegeman, Katy. (Mrs. Paul Wegeman). See Rudolph, Katy.

Wegeman, Keith. DU champion; U.S. Olympic team; Instructor U. S. Army Mountain and Cold Weather Program. CSHF

Wegeman, Paul. Outstanding jr. at Steamboat Springs; Olympian, 1952.   CSHF.

Welch, Tom. One of the founders of Crested Butte.

Werner, Gladys "Skeeter." Steamboat Springs 1950 jr. nat. champion; FIS 1953; Olympian, 1956; Nat. Veterans champion, 1970;   CSHF.

Werner, Loris. Steamboat Springs nat. jr. champion, 1958; WSC NCAA Skimeister Award, 1965, 1966; U.S. nat. champion, 1965; Olympian, 1968; National Veterans champion, 1970; Steamboat Springs manager and instructor.

Werner, Wallace "Buddy." Steamboat Springs nat. jr. champion, 1952; U.S. nat. champion, 1957, 1959; CU NCAA slalom and Alpine combined champion, 1961, 1963; first American to win a major European downhill event, Hahnenhamm, Austria, 1962; also won Grand Prix Chamonix, 1954, 1956; Holmenkollen, 1962; Lauberhorn, 1958; Criterium of the First Snow, 1963; Roch Cup, 1959, 1961; Holmenkollen Kandahar, 1954, 1956, 1962; Harriman Cup, 1961, 1963; Nat. Ski Hall of Fame Athlete of the Year, 1959; Silver Belt, 1959; Schoenberger Award, 1964; Beck Trophy, 1956, 1957, 1958; White Stag Trophy, 1959, 1963; FIS, 1956, 1963; Olympian, 1956, 1964; widely recognized for promotion of international understanding in the skiing sport; killed in Swiss avalanche, April 12, 1964; CSHF; NSHF; Colorado Sports Hall of Fame; Mount Werner, Steamboat Springs, named in his memory; also in his memory, Buddy Werner Ski Program for youth, Steamboat Springs library, award for outstanding skiing and international understanding.

White, Louise. Fort Collins pioneer skier who established Colorado Skiing Association for women; U.S. Amateur Ski Association downhill, slalom and combined, 1937; helped promote Idledale area; CSHF.

Wiik, Birgitta. Steamboat Springs and WSC champion skier; NCAA X-C champion; WSC women's coach.

Wiik, Sven. WSC coach, 1949-69; FIS coach, 1958, 1960; Olympic X-C coach, 1960; "Patriarch of Colorado Cross-country Skiing;" founded Scandanavian Lodge and Nordic touring center, Steamboat Springs; with Billy Kidd; developed first international Special Olympics for skiing, 1976; CSHF.

Williams, Elizabell. Leader in establishing ski programs for disabled children. CSHF

Wilmot, Leonn C. "Wil." 10th Mountain Division. Founded Ski Broadmoor; Halstead Award. CSHF

Willoughby, Frank and Fred. Helped build Ajax Mountain trails at Aspen and original jump there. CSHF.

Windisch, Erich. Veteran ski instructor, Vail. Co-director Arapahoe Basin; CSC-USA instructor of the year. CSHFK

Wingle, Pete. U.S. Forest Service Regional Director of Recreation; established favorable cooperation between ski areas and National Forests; organized the first National Avalanche School. CSHF.

Woods, Len. 10th Mt. Div.; Aspen ski instructor.

Wren, George. Early skiing mail carrier, Steamboat Springs area; great uncle of Gordon Wren.

Wren, Gordon "Gordy." Steamboat Springs member of Colorado's winning Jeffers Cup team, 1939; 10th Mt. Div.; Aspen instructor; first American to jump over 300 feet; only American to qualify in all four Olympic skiing events; Olympian, 1948; Harriman Cup, 1942; Nat. Nordic champion, 1949; manager of Howelson Hill; directed Steamboat Springs jr. program and coached school team; manager, Jackson Hole, Wyoming; coach, Reno, Nevada; mountaineering instructor, Fort Carson; manager, Mount Werner; a founder of Steamboat Lake area; Layman Trophy, 1949; U.S. Nordic coach, 1949; Nat. Veterans champion, 1963; CSHF; NSFH; Colorado Sports Hall of Fame.

Wright, Dick. 10th Mt. Div.; later Aspen instructor.

Wright, Paul W. "Frosty." Director of Athletics, WSC, who was designated "Founder of National Intercollegiate Skiing" by NCAA as a result of long promotion to include skiing in its contests; served on original NCAA rules committee.

Yeager, Ron. CU Champion; U.S. X-C team, 1972; Olympian, 1972, 1976.

Young, Bob. Promoter of Adam's Rib area.

Zoline, Joe. Promoter of Telluride.

APPENDIX II: WHAT WAS WHERE?

This is a guide to the general locations of ski areas past, present, and proposed, in Colorado.

Adam's Rib. Near Eagle. Delayed in approval for development.

Ajax Mountain. Earlier name of Aspen Mountain; opened 1938.

Allenspark. Sixteen miles south of Estes Park; developed 1947.

Altenback. See Geneva Basin.

Arapahoe Basin (A Basin). West side of Loveland Pass; opened 1947.

Arapahoe East. Ten miles west of Denver at Mount Vernon Canyon; opened in 1971; also known as Ski Golden.

Arroehead. West of Beaver Creek.

Ashcroft. Twelve miles south of Aspen; large area proposed, 1937; site of Stewart Mace's sled dogs and ski touring; its Hayden Peak proposal rejected; some rope tow skiing in summer.

Aspen Heights. Ski area on Grand Mesa, 1937.

Aspen Highlands. Large area near Aspen.

Aspen Mountain. Later name of Ajax; opened 1947.

Beaver Creek. Near Avon, west of Vail, opened 1980.

Beaver Meadows. West of Fort Collins.

Berthoud Pass. North of Georgetown on U.S. 40; earliest documented Colorado rope tow, 1937; nation's first double chairlift, 1947.

Breckenridge. On Colorado 9 between Dillon and Fairplay; opened 1961.

Broadmoor (Ski Broadmoor). South of Colorado Springs; opened 1961.

Buttermilk. Just west of Aspen; developed in 1960s.

Cameron Pass. On Colorado 14, twenty-eight miles southwest of Walden, started 1938.

Cardinal Hill. At Nederland.

Cedar Hill. Near Paonia; opened 1942.

Cemetery Hill. Near Dillon; inundated by Lake Dillon.

Chapman Hill. Northeast of Durango.

Climax. On Colorado 91 atop Fremont Pass, between Leadville and Dillon; opened 1936.

Conquistador. Five miles west of Westcliffe; junction Colorado 69 and 96; opened 1936.

Cooper Hill (Ski Cooper). Atop Tennessee Pass on U.S. 24, ten miles from Leadville; original Camp Hale area, 1942.

Copper Mountain. On Wheeler Flats just east of Vail Pass; junction of Interstate 70 and Colorado 91; opened 1973.

Crag Crest. National Ski Trail atop Grand Mesa; southeast of Grand Junction.

Cranor Hill. Three miles north of Gunnison.

Creede. On Colorado 149 between Del Norte and Lake City; opened 1964.

Crested Butte. Three miles from Crested Butte; just off Colorado 135; opened 1963.

Cuchara Valley Resort. Near La Veta; formerly Panadero.

Cupula Hill. Overlooks Western State College, Gunnison; operated briefly in 1930s.

Dallas Divide. On Colorado 62, twelve miles west of Ridgway.

Deer Mountain. Near Tiny Town, 1930s.

Devil's Hangover. Once popular X-C training area on west slope of Rabbit Ears Pass near Steamboat Springs.

Devil's Thumb. Ski touring resort near Fraser.

Dillon. Prestrud jump on Interstate 70, 10 miles west of Eisenhower Tunnel; first jump built in 1914.

Eldora (Lake Eldora). Twenty-one miles west of Boulder via Colorado 119; ski area since 1917.

Emerald Mountain. Above Howelson Hill, Steamboat Springs; opened about 1947; closed soon after that.

Estes Park. Name for former Hidden Valley.

Evergreen. Proposed area southwest of Denver on Colorado 74; lack of funding in 1965 stopped development.

Fawn Valley. East of Paonia on Colorado 133; no longer exists.

Forest Lakes. Near Bayfield, north on U.S. 160.

Fraser Valley. Near Fraser, west of U.S. 40.

Frosty Basin. Former ski tow near Granby.

Fun Valley. Near Littleton on Deer Creek Road; opened 1968; later closed.

Genesee Mountain. Fifteen miles west of Denver along Interstate 70.

Geneva Basin. North of Grant on Guanella Pass Road; also called Indianhead; recently renamed Altenbach.

Glen Cove. Early area in Pike National Forest west of Colorado Springs; developed 1939.

Glenwood Mountain Park. Above Red Mountain, Glenwood Springs; operated 1965-1966 only.

Golden (Ski Golden). Former name for Arapahoe East.

Guanella Pass. South of Georgetown.

Hesperus. Near town of Hesperus, thirteen miles west of Durango, on U.S. 160.

Hidden Valley. Former name for Ski Estes Park.

Hideaway Park. North of Winter Park; site of English-style resort, "The Coachman;" opened 1963.

Holliday Hill. South of Glenwood Springs; early name for Sunlight.

Homewood Park. Near Tiny Town, southwest of Denver on U.S. 285.

Hoosier Pass. Between Breckenridge and Alma.

Hot Sulphur Springs. Colorado's first sport skiing area, on U.S. 40 in Middle Park; opened 1911; redeveloped 1947.

Howelson Hill. Overlooks Steamboat Springs; developed 1915; completely rebuild 1974.

Idlewild. A former part of the modern town of Winter Park on U.S. 40; opened 1960.

Indianhead Mountain. North of Grant; now Geneva Basin; opened 1961.

Jones Pass. Historic ski area near Empire, above the Moffat Tunnel.

Jumbo Run. On Grand Mesa, 1939-1941.

Kendall Mountain. At Silverton.

Keystone. On U.S. 6 on west slope of Loveland Pass; opened 1970.

Lake Catamount. Proposed area on west slope of Rabbit Ears Pass.

Lake City. At Lake City on Colorado 149.

Loveland Basin. On U.S. 6 on east side of Loveland Pass, just off Interstate 70; originally skied in 1920s; established area in late 1930s.

Marble. Near town of Marble, eight miles east of Colorado 133.

Mary Jane. At Winter Park.

Meadow Mountain. West Vail, near Minturn; started 1967.

Mesa Creek Ski Course. On Grand Mesa, 1950s.

Michaelson's Ranch. Near Collbran; "Tough" ski run in 1940s.

Monarch (Ski Monarch).   Near Garfield, on east side of Monarch Pass, just off U.S. 50; early area; tow, 1939; developed, 1956.

North Peak. New area near Keystone.

Old Sam (Mount Sampson). Above Cedaredge about 1949.

Ouray. North of town of Ouray on U.S. 550.

Panadero. Eleven miles south of La Veta on Colorado 12; former name of Cuchara Valley Resort.

Peaceful Valley. Between Lyons and Estes Park on U.S. 36.

Pikes Peak. Twenty-five miles west of Colorado Springs on U.S. 24.

Pioneer. On Cement Creek, twenty miles north of Gunnison; first Colorado chair lift, 1938; closed, 1951.

Porcupine Gulch. Old ski run near present Keystone.

Powderhorn.   North slope of Grand Mesa, thirty-five miles southeast of Grand Junction on Colorado 85; opened under that name in 1966.

Prestrud Jump. See Dillon.

Purgatory. Fifty miles north of Durango on U.S. 550; opened 1967.

Quick's Hill. Earlier name for Rozman Hill, Crested Butte.

Raton-Sugarite. Southeast of Trinidad on New Mexico line.

Red Mountain. Overlooks Glenwood Springs; opened 1941; closed 1966.

Red Mountain. Cross-country ski resort near U.S. 550 between Ouray and Silverton.

Rilliet Hill. Historic area on west slope of Lookout Mountain near Golden in 1920s.

Rimrock. Cross-country course on Grand Mesa.

Rollins Pass. West of Pinecliffe, near east portal of the Moffat Tunnel; begun 1962.

Rozman Hill. On Colorado 135, three miles south of Crested Butte; 1930s area; revived 1950s.

Sagebrush Hill. One mile west of Gunnison; abandoned 1930s.

San Isabel (Ski San Isabel). Twenty miles from Rye on Colorado 165.

Seven Utes. Ski touring area twenty-eight miles east of Walden, Colorado 14.

Sharktooth. Six miles west of Greeley near U.S. 34; opened 1971.

Silver Creek. Near Grandy; opened 1983; noted for family skiing.

Silver Hills. Thirty-eight miles west of Pueblo on Colorado 96.

Silver Tip Ranch. Original site of Keystone.

Silverton (Kendall Mountain). Near Silverton; begun as new development on 1962.

Ski Trail Mountain. Between Granby and Grand Lake, 100 miles west of Denver.

Snodgrass Mountain. Proposed extension of Crested Butte area.

Snow King. Early ski area near Hot Sulphur Springs.

Squaw Pass. Thirty miles west of Denver; opened 1963.

St. Mary's Glacier. Fall River exit, Interstate 70, Fifty-four miles west of Denver.

Stagecoach. South of Steamboat Springs; begun 1973; abandoned.

Steamboat Lake. Eleven miles northwest of Steamboat Springs; abandoned.

Steamboat Ski Area. Later name for Mount Werner and Storm Mountain.

Stoner. Former ski area on Colorado 145, twenty-seven miles northeast of Cortez.

Storm Mountain. Earlier name for Mount Werner and Steamboat.

Sunlight. Eight miles south of Glenwood Springs; opened 1966.

Tamarron. Resort twenty-one miles north of Durango on U.S. 550.

Telluride. Near Telluride on Colorado 145; opened 1972.

Tenderfoot Mountain (Cripple Creek). Near Cripple Creek; opened 1949.

Tenderfoot Mountain (Gunnison). Now "W" Mountain; overlooks Gunnison; site of 1886 race.

Top O' La Veta. Atop La Veta Pass, U.S. 160 between La Veta and Fort Garland; opened 1959.

Twin Sisters. Eight miles south of Glenwood Springs; opened 1966.

Vail. West side of Vail Pass on Interstate 70, 100 miles west of Denver; opened 1962.

Vasquez. New area at Winter Park; opened 1984.

Werner (Mount Werner). Earlier name for Steamboat Ski Area.

West Portal. Historic area at west end of Moffat Tunnel.

Westcliffe. Earlier name for Coronado area, near Westcliffe.

White Pine. Ghost town northwest of Monarch Pass; rope tow in 1930s.

Winter Park. North of Berthoud Pass on U.S. 40.

Wolf Creek Pass. East of Pagosa Springs on U.S. 160.

Wolf Creek Valley Resort. Proposed area west of Wolf Creek Pass.

Woodchuck Hill. Early jumping site at west end of Steamboat Springs.

APPENDIX III: WHAT WAS WHAT?

The following is a selected list of historical ski races, awards, and organizations.

Arlberg Club. Early Denver ski club.

Arlberg Kandahar. Slalom races held at five European resorts.

Beck International Trophy. Founded by George Beck in 1930; awarded each year to best U.S. skier in international competition.

Bietila Trophy (Paul Bietila Trophy). Annual award to the American-born skier scoring highest in national ski jumping.

Blegen Award (Julius Blegen Memorial Plaque and Medal). Named for the former treasurer of the National Ski Association; U.S. Olympic coach in 1932; presented to association member who has contributed outstanding service to the sport.

Buddy Werner League. Sort of a "little league of skiing," this program fosters instruction for youths aged nine to thirteen.

Burton Trophy (Gale Cotton Burton Memorial Trophy). Award for fifteen to eighteen kilometer national X-C winner.

Colorado Mountain Club. Organization founded in Denver, 1912, with branches in other cities; instrumental in pioneering ski clubs and associations.

Colorado Passenger Tramway Safety Board. Organization founded to establish standards for ski lifts and other conveyances.

Colorado Ski Country USA. Promotional organization for Colorado ski areas.

Colorado Ski Hall of Fame (CSHF). Colorado's highest honor in the sport; hall located at the ski museum in Vail.

Criterium of the First Snow. First major European race held each year; held at Val d'Isere, France.

Equitable Family Ski Challenge. Family group racing teams complete; the youngest must be under nineteen years old.

Eskimo Club. Early Denver ski organization.

Federation Internationale de Ski (FIS). International ski meet held yearly until 1950; later alternated with Olympics on four-year cycles.

Finlandia Trophy. Awarded to outstanding U.S. X-C skier each year.

First of Denver Cup. Winter Park professional race.

Galstead Memorial Award. Given by the Rocky Mountain Ski Association for outstanding contribution to the sport of skiing.

Gelande. Contest in which jumping skiers must use standard skis and poles, as opposed to Nordic skis and no poles in regular jump meets.

Golden Quill Award. Citation for outstanding skiing publicity.

Grand Prix du Megeve. Famed European international race.

Hahnenkamm Races. Annual contest, since 1933, held on mountain of that name overlooking Kitzbuhel, Austria.

halstead Memorial Award. By USSA Rocky Mountain Division for outstanding service to skiing.

Harriman Cup. Individual award in annual races at Sun Valley.

Hirsch Award (Harold S. Hirsch Award). Silver-plated typewriter presented for superb sport writing on skiing.

Holmenkollen. At Oslo, Norway, the world's oldest regular championship contest on national and international levels; awards Crown Prince Cup and King's Cup.

Holmenkollen-Kandahar. International Norwegian slalom meet.

International Ski Racers Association. Professional ski racing circuit.

International Speed Skiing Association. Organization conducting races for both individual and team competition.

Jeffers Cup. Ski team races held at Sun Valley, Idaho.

Junior Races. Races for skiers under age nineteen.

Kandahar. Slalom race named for English victory in Afghan town by that name in 1800s; original at St. Anton, Switzerland, but name used world-wide for such contests.

Lange Cup. Award in professional skiing.

Lauberhorn. Originally only for British and Swiss ski racers; now international meet held at Wengen, Switzerland.

Layman Trophy (Paul Nash Laymen, Jr. Trophy). Award to winner of national Nordic combined competition.

Master Ski Series. Successor to National Veterans' Races.

National Collegiate Athletic Association (NCAA). Nation's highest level intercollegiate skiing contests begun in 1954.

National Ski Areas Association. Organization of area operators.

National Ski Championships. Meets for amateur skiers, including junior and veterans meets; operated by U.S. Ski Association.

National Ski Hall of Fame (NSHF). Highest U.S. honor in skiing achievement; located at Ishpeming, Michigan.

National Ski Hall of Fame Athlete of the Year Award. An award for outstanding performance by a skier not yet inducted into the Hall of Fame.

National Ski Patrol. U.S. organization which establishes standards, supervises training, and maintains rosters for ski patrols.

National Standard Ski Race (NASTAR). Begun in 1968 by **Ski** magazine, nation wide competition based on general records, and allowing qualification on various areas, eliminating need for a specific site.

National Veterans Races. Competition for older skiers, age twenty-seven and up, in five different classifications of age.

Olympics, Winter. Begun in 1924; held in winter preceding regular Summer Olympics.

Professional Skier of the Year Award. **Ski** magazine cup given annually to the top money winner in professional racing.

Roch Cup. Annual Aspen race named for Andre Roch.

Rocky Mountain Intercollegiate Association (RMIA). Sponsors races annually at various ski areas.

Rocky Mountain Ski Association (RMSA). Organization which grew out of Southern RMSA to coordinate plans and meets of ski clubs.

Schoenberger Award. Citation to University of Colorado skier, given annually in memory of Dick Schoenberger.

Silver Belt Trophy. Originally awarded in Sierra competition as early as 1854; revived as national spring meet in 1940.

Skimiester Award. Citation for best all-around performance given by several ski racing organizations.

Ski Writers Award. Annual presentation for best journalistic coverage of skiing.

Southern Rocky Mountain Ski Association (SRMSA). Established in late 1930s to promote ski competition among clubs in Wyoming, Colorado, and New Mexico.

Vail Cup. Award in annual racing meet at Vail.

Werner Award (Wallace "Bud" Werner Award). Presented every year to outstanding U.S. skier who has also made a significant contribution to international goodwill.

Western State Invitational. Hosted by Western State College, this meet at Crested Butte was an annual "bell-weather" meet for area collegiate teams.

White Band. Slalom race meet at St. Mortiz, Switzerland.

White Stag Trophy. Awarded nationally to winners of ladies' combined downhill, slalom and giant slalom, and to men's Alpine combined race winners.

World Cup. Season-long annual international competition open to all racers.

Zipfelberger Club. Early Denver ski club.

Selected Bibliography

BOOKS:

Abraham, Horst. Skiing Right. San Francisco: Harper and Row, 1983.

Beattie, Bob. Beattie's Guide to Ski Racing. Denver: Award House, 1971.

Berry, I. William. The Great North American Ski Book. New York: Charles Scribner's Sons, 1982.

Blair, Edward. Leadville, Colorado's Magic City. Boulder, Colo: Pruett Publishing Co., 1980.

Borneman, Walter R. Marshall Pass. Colorado Springs: Century One Press, 1980.

Bowen, Ezra. The Book of American Skiing. Philadelphia: J.P. Lippincott Co., 1963.

Brower, David R. Editor, Manual of Ski Mountaineering. Berkeley: University of California Press, 1947.

Burroughs, John Rolfe. "I Never Look Back": The Story of Buddy Werner. Boulder, Colo: Johnson Publishing Co., 1967.

Ski Town USA. Steamboat Springs, Colo.: Pilot Press, 1962.

Burton, Hal. The Ski Troops. New York: Simon and Schuster, 1971.

Casewit, Curtis W. Ski Racing: Advice by the Experts. New York: Arco Publishing Co., 1963.

Colorado Sports Hall of Fame. Colorado, The Superstar State. Baton Rouge, La.: Moran Publishing Co., 1979.

Coquoz, Rene L. The Invisible Men on Skis. Boulder, Colo.: Johnson Publishing Co., 1970.

Dallas, Sandra. Vail. Boulder, Colo.: Pruett Publishing Co., 1969.

Dercum, Edna Strand. "It's Easy, Edna, It's Downhill All The Way." Dillon, Colo.: Sirpos Press, 1981.

Dole, Minot. Adventures in Skiing. New York: Franklin Watts, Inc., 1965.

Dyer, John Lewis. The Snow-Shoe Itinerant. Cincinnati: Cranston and Stowe, 1891.

Eriksen, Stein. Come Ski With Me. Ed. Martin Luray. New York: Bonanza Books, 1966.

Fetter, Richard and Suzanne. Telluride - From Pick to Powder. Caldwell, Idaho: Caxton Printers, 1979.

Fiester, Mark. Blasted, Beloved Breckenridge. Boulder, Colo.: Pruett Publishing Co., 1973.

Gardiner, Charles Fox. Doctor at Timberline. Caldwell, Idaho: Caxton Printers, 1938.

Gibbons, James Joseph. In the San Juan, Colorado: Sketches. Chicago: Calumet Book and Engraving Co., 1898.

Gilliland, Mary Ellen. Summit: A Gold Rush History of Summit County, Colorado. Silverthorn, Colo.: Alpenrose Press, 1980.

Hovelsen, Leif. The Flying Idea. Norman: University of Oklahoma Press, 1975.

Jay, John, and John and Frankie O'Rear. Ski Down the Years. New York: Award House, 1966.

Liebers, Arthur. The Complete Book of Winter Sports. New York: Coward McCann, Inc., 1963.

Lund, Morton, et. al. The Ski Book. New York: Arbor House, 1982.

Mann, Bob "Boogie." Hot Dog Skiing. New York: W.W. Norton, 1973.

Mumie, Nolie. History of Tin Cup, Colorado (Virginia City). Boulder, Colo.: Johnson Publishing Co., 1963.

Needham, Richard. Editor, Ski Magazine's Encyclopedia of Skiing. (Revised and enlarged.) New York: Harper and Row, 1979.

O'Rear, John and Frankie. The Aspen Story. New York: A.S. Barnes and Co., 1966.

Pote, Winston. Mountain Troops: Camp Hale, Colorado. Camden, Maine: Down East Books, 1980.

Pratt, John Lowell, and Jim Benagh. The Official Encyclopedia of Sports. New York: Franklin Watts, In., 1965.

Richards, Dee. Steamboat Round the Bend. Steamboat Springs, Colo.: Steamboat Pilot, 1976.

Scharff, Robert. Editor, Ski Magazine's Enclclopedia of Skiing. New York: Harper and Row, 1970.

Sibley, George. Park of a Winter. New York: Harmony Books, 1978.

Smith, Duane A. A Rocky Mountain Boom Town: A History of Durango. Albuquerque: University of New Mexico Press, 1980.

Urquhart, Lena M. Glenwood Springs: Spa in the Mountains. Boulder, Colo.: Pruett Publishing Co., 1970.

Wallace, Betty. Gunnison Country. Denver: Sage Books, 1960.

Wentworth, Frank L. Aspen on the Roaring Fork. Lakewood, Colo.: Francis B. Rizzari, 1950.

Wiik, Sven, and David Sumner. The Regnery Guide to Ski Touring. Chicago: Henry Regnery Co., 1974.

Wren, Jean. Steamboat Springs and the "Treacherous and Speedy Skee." Steamboat Springs, Colo.: Steamboat Pilot, 1972.

ARTICLES IN PERIODICALS:

Benson, Jack A. "Before Skiing Was Fun." **Western Historical Quarterly**, VIII:4 (October; 1977).

Colorado Graphic, April 18, 1891. "Snowshoe Post-Routes." Reprinted in **Colorado Magazine**, XVII:1 (January 1940).

Cornwall, Harry. "My First Year in the Gunnison Country." (ed. By Duane Vandenbusche) **Colorado Magazine,** XLVI:3 (Summer 1969).

Denison, Alice. "Pioneering Near Steamboat Springs, 1885-1886." **Colorado Magazine**, XXVIII:2 (Aprin 1951).

Dresbeck, LeRoy J. "The Ski: Its History and Historiography." **Technology and Culture,** VIII (October 1967).

Dunway, Bill. "Skiing Personality: The Lift Maker." **National Skiing**, November 15, 1954.

Foster, Mark S. "Colorado's Defeat of the 1976 Winter Olympics." **Colorado Magazine**, LIII:2 (Spring 1976).

Greiner, Jean M. "An Early Colorado Gondola." **Colorado Magazine**, L:3 (Summer 1973).

Hafen, LeRoy R. "A Winter March Across the Rockies." **Colorado Magazine**, IV:1 (January 1927).

Hastings, James K. "A Winter in the High Mountains, 1871-72." **Colorado Magazine**, XXVII:3 (July 1950).

Hermann, Heinz. "The Case Against the Ski Tow." **Colorado Quarterly**, XXIV (Spring 1954).

Lund, Morton. "The Many Visions of Willy Schaeffler." **Ski Magazine**, October 1967.

Quillen, Ed. "Monarch Began as a WPA Project." **Winter Fun** (Salida), 1981-82.

Rand, Abby. "Where Kids and Kidd are King." **Ski Magazine**, January 1983.

Smith, Bob. "I Am a T-Bar." **Skier**, November 1963.

Steward, Doug. "Haven at the Summit." **Colorado Life**, 6:2 (March/April 1984).

Walker, Leslie. "Powderhorn: On Our Way Up." **Directions**, The Magazine for Western Colorado, Winter 1982.

Warren, E.R. "Snow-shoeing in the Rocky Mountains." **Outing**, IX (January 1887).

GOVERNMENT AND ORGANIZATIONAL BULLETINS:

Colorado Ski Country USA. Summary: Economic Impacts of Skiing in Colorado. Denver, 1982.

Dwyer, Charles F. Aerial Tramways, Ski Lifts, and Tows: Descriptive and Terminology. Washington, D.C., U.S. Department of Agriculture, Forest Service, June 1975.

Hauk, Paul. Ski Area Chronology. Various historical reports on ski areas in White River National Forest. Glenwood Springs: White River National Forest.

Perla, Ronald I., and M. Martinelli, Jr. Avalanche Handbook, Washington, D.C.: U.S. Department of Agriculture, Forest Service, July 1976.

Welles, Barbara C. Snowpack Augmentation Research Needs: A History of Weather Modification in Colorado. Denver: Colorado Department of Natural Resources, 1982.

MANUSCRIPTS AND OTHER UNPUBLISHED MATERIALS:

Blickensderfer, J.C. Reminiscences of Skiing in Colorado, 1922-1968. Typescript, Hart Library, Colorado Historical Society, Denver.

Douglas, John F. Developed Sites (Monarch Park Winter Sports Area). Pueblo: San Isable National Forest, February 20, 1960.

Gunnison County Scrapbook, Paonia Public Library, Paonia, Colorado.

Koster, Wallace. Letter to Georgia Lodders, December 13, 1983.

Moore, King. An Essay on the History of the Western State Hiking and Outing Club. Typescript, Western State College, Gunnison, July 15, 1968.

O'Neil, Kimberly. Zip-N-Walk a Mile (Cupula Hill). Typescript, Western State College, Gunnison, 1980.

Sherman, Gary J. I Forgot My Parachute. Typescript, Western State College, Gunnison, 1977.

Snyder, Hubert L. Organization of High School Skiing. Unpublished M.A. Thesis, Western State College, Gunnison, 1956.

Strobuck, Marilyn. The Sagebrush Hill: Left to the Wind. Typescript, Western State College, Gunnison, 1980.

Taylor, Clara D. A Brief History of Irwin, A Ghost Town. Unpublished M.A. Thesis, Western State College, Gunnison, 1930.

Toll, Henry W. Memo to Georgia Lodders, January 20, 1983.

NEWSPAPERS AND OTHER PERIODICALS

Aspen Daily Times, 1936-1980.

Cervi's Journal, 1960-1970.

Colorado and the Rocky Mountain West, 1969-1980.

Colorado State Normal School Newsletter, (Western State College), 1916-1917.

Delta County Independent, 1984.

Denver Post, 1935-1983.

Denver Rocky Mountain News, 1953-1983.

Durango Weekly Herald, 1935-1939.

Glenwood Springs Post, 1983-1984.

Grand Junction Daily Sentinel, 1983-1984.

Gunnison News-Champion, 1920-1970.

Leadville Herald-Democrat, 1940-1950.

Leadville Carbondale Chronicle, 1942-1944.

Steamboat Pilot, 1913-1933, 1983-1984.

Summit County Journal, 1983-1984.

Summit Sentinel, 1980-1984.

Wall Street Journal, 1983-1984.

COLLEGE PRESS RELEASES:

University of Colorado, 1956-1983.

University of Denver, 1954-1978.

Western State College of Colorado, 1970-1983.

MUSEUMS:

Aspen: Stoddard House.

Littleton: Kandahar Restaurant and Ski Museum.

Steamboat Springs: Tread of the Pioneers Museum.

Vail: Colorado Ski Museum and Hall of Fame.

PERSONAL INTERVIEWS:

David M. Abbott, at Denver, December 31, 1982.

John Burritt, near Hotchkiss, January 23, 1983.

Charles Dwyer, at Lakewood, March 30, 1983.

Allison Gooding, at Steamboat Springs, September 22, 1983.

Paul Hauk, at Glenwood Springs, November 7, 1983.

Dale Hollingsworth, at Grand Junction, February 12, 1984.

James Holme, at Indian Hills, March 31, 1983.

Lief Hovelsen, at Vail, December 13, 1982.

Steve Knowlton, at Littleton, March 31, 1983.

Rial Lake, at Gunnison, June 23, 1983.

Georgia Lodders, at Denver, March 30, 1983.

James Prendergast, at Paonia, February 2, 1983.

Sven Wiik, at Steamboat Springs, February 12, 1983.

Gordon Wren, at Steamboat Springs, February 13, 1983.

Jean Wren, at Steamboat Springs, February 13, 1983.

Paul Zahradka, at Gunnison, June 22, 1983.

ACKNOWLEDGEMENTS

The author wishes to express his sincere thanks to the many people who gave him valuable research information, allowed him time for interviews, and read the manuscript in its preparation.

Library staffs who helped were those of the Stephen H. Hart Library, Colorado Historical Society; Western History Collection of the Denver Public Library; Colorado Mountain Club Library; Vail Public Library; Paonia Public Library; Buddy Werner Memorial Library at Steamboat Springs; Gunnison and Western State College libraries; Mesa County and Mesa College libraries. The staff of Colorado Ski Country USA were very helpful; also the publicity staffs of Western State College, and the Universities of Colorado and Denver.

Walt Borneman of Evergreen edited the original manuscript. Dede Fay of Grandby made a great contribution to this revision.

A very special thanks to Loreen Katz, curator of the Colorado Ski Museum and Hall of Fame, Vail, for help in revision and updating of material. Individuals who did much to help in the progress of research on this work include, from the Denver area: David Abbott, James Holme, Steve Knowlton, Charles Dwyer and Georgia Lodders; in Boulder, Professor Lee Scamehorn; and in Vail, Pamela Horan-Kates and Donald Simonton.

Jean and Gordon Wren at Steamboat Springs provided much insight, as did Sven Wiik. In Glenwood Springs, Paul Hauk; and in Hot Sulphur Springs, Bob Black.

At Gunnison, Rial Lake, Mickey Zahradka and J.W. Campbell; at Leadville, Disa Meldrum; and at Westcliffe, Robyn Milstein.

At Delta, Marilyn Howard, Doug Stewart, Geri Morris and Polly Hammer; and in Paonia, Jim Prendergast and Esther Johnson, and at Austin, Genevive Hice.

A special thanks must go to Leif Hovelsen, from Oslo, Norway, for his insights into the career of his famous father, Carl Howelsen

To his own daughter and sons, all accomplished skiers, the writer owes much thanks. To his wife, who accompanied him on several thousand miles of travel for research, pondered over every word of the manuscript, and maintained the glow of creative inspiration for more than two years of work, the author can find no words adequate to express his deep appreciation.

INDEX

Aas, Morton 14

Abbott, David 143

Abbott, Dudley 143

Adam's Rib 119, 165

Adams State College 103

Adgate, Cary 143

Ahern, Pat 143

Air Force Academy 106

Aitkin, Leonard 143

Ajax Mountain 52, 68, 165

Allen, "Skip" 93, 113

Allens Park 53, 85, 165

Alma 9, 12

Alta, Utah 5

Altenbach 165

American Cement Corporation 96

American Skiing 48

Anderson, Chet 99, 100, 144

Arapahoe Basin 65, 79, 81, 99, 109, 165

Arapahoe East 199, 165

Arlberg, Austria 3

Arlberg Club 29, 32, 100, 171

Arlberg Kandahar 171

Armstrong, John 12, 144

Arnold, Landis 144

Arrowhead 165

Arstal, Henning 144

Ashcroft 48, 50, 58, 119

Ashley, Frank 41, 70, 144

Aspen 17, 49, 50, 51, 60, 65-77, 103, 137, 139

Aspen Heights 165

Aspen Highlands 65, 75, 125, 165

Aspen Institute 65, 75

Aspen Mountain 69, 74, 165

Aspen Music Festival 75

Aspen Ski Corporation 75, 95, 96

Atwater, Monty 144

Aurora Ski Club (California) 3

Avalanches 125-126

Avon 113, 177

Baar, Ron 144

Baar, Myke 74, 144

Bailey, John 95, 144

Baker, Jim 7

Balch, Bob 37, 43, 59, 63, 144

Bald Mountain 96

Balfanz, John 144

Bancroft, Albert 31, 144

Banks, John 144

Barrows, Jim "Moose" 84, 144

Barwise, Norman 144

Bass, Harry 144

Baum, Harry Jr. 95, 144

Bayer, Herbert 68, 144

Bayer, Seth 144

Beattie, Bob 106, 144

Beaver Creek 113, 117, 119, 138, 165

Beaver Meadows 165

Bechtold, Carl 144

Beck Trophy 171

Bietila Trophy 171

Bellmar, Fred C. 39, 145

Benedict, Fritz 65, 96, 135, 145

Berge, Trgve   145

Berger, George Jr.   145

Berger, Miriam   145

Berlin, N. H.   3

Berry, Ray & Josephine   83

Berthoud Pass   36, 40, 41, 43, 55, 81, 199, 165

Big Dipper Run   48

Billings, Norton   145

Blaurock, Carl   28

Blegen Award   171

Blickensderfer, J. C.   37, 40, 145

Blistered Horn Mine   48

Boehm, Karl   65, 145

Boettcher, Charles   37, 145

Bookstrom, Hans M.   145

Borkovec, Steve   145

Boulder   31

Bowles, James A.   95, 145

Boyce, Kelly   52, 145

Boyce, Paul   145

Bradley, Packer   83

Bradley, Steve   48, 81, 106, 145

Branch, Tom   145

Braun, Alfred   145

Bray, Andy   145

Breckenridge   9, 52, 65, 70, 95, 137, 145, 165

Briner, Gordon   145

Briner, John   145

Broadmoor   47, 65, 89, 126, 165

Brookshank, Scott   146

Brown, D. R. C.   52, 69, 73, 146

Brown, Frank   146

Brown, William R.   90

Buddy Werner League   171

Bulkley, Frank   37, 39, 146

Burritt, John   135, 146

Burton Trophy   171

Buttermilk   65, 70, 75, 165

Button, Horace   22, 53, 146

Butts, Dave   146

California Gulch   9

Callaway, Howard   93, 124, 146

Cameron Pass   165

Camp Hale   55, 57-65, 67, 79, 81, 130

Carbondale   103

Cardinal Hill   165

Cedar Hill   165

Cedaredge   55

Cement Creek   43

Cemetery Hill   95, 165

Chaffee, Rick   146

Chamonix, France   5

Chapman Hill   55, 166

Chase, Curt   65, 146

Christensen, Peik   146

Civilian Conservation Corps   36, 43

Clark, Gen. Mark   63

Clayton, Dr. Mack L.   146

Climax   18, 55, 83, 103, 165

Climax Molybdenum Co.   55, 93, 95

Colo, Zeno   74

Colorado A. M. College   103, 106

Colorado College   103, 106

Colorado Mountain Club   27, 29, 31, 32, 41, 171

Colorado Passenger Tramway Safety Board 171

Colorado Rocky Mountain School   103

Colorado School of Mines   103, 106

Colorado Ski Country U. S. A.   65, 121, 171

Colorado Ski Hall of Fame   28, 121

Colorado Ski Museum   121

Colorado Skiing Association   55

Colorado Springs   31

Colorado State College (University of Northern Colorado)   103

Colorado State University   103

Colorado, University of   97, 103, 106

Comstam, E. G.   43, 130, 146

Conquistador   120, 165

Cooper Hill (Ski Cooper)   63, 83, 165

Coors, Adolph III   146

Copper Mountain   113, 115, 138, 166

Cornwall, Harry C.   15, 146

Cotton, Ken   146

Couch, Edmond Jr.   146

Crag Crest Trail   135, 166

Cranmer, George   43, 48, 146

Cranor Hill   101, 166

Crawford, Gary   84, 146

Crawford, Marvin   84, 96, 99, 146

Creede   53, 85, 166

Cress, Jennings   146

Cress, John   146

Crested Butte   4, 15, 17, 19, 47, 89, 90, 93, 124, 138

Cripple Creek   85

Criterium of the First Snow   171

Crystal   15

Cuchara Valley Resort   120, 166

Cullman, Duncan   147

Cumbres Pass   53

Cunningham, Gerry   65, 147

Cupula Hill   166

Dahle, Gunnar   26, 147

d' Albizi, Lt.   31, 147

Dallas Divide   101, 166

Dalpes, James Louis   28

Darley, George M.   13, 147

Dartmouth College   4, 35

Davis, Wilfred "Slim"   53, 84, 147

Deer Mountain   166

Delta   55

Demers, Eddie   147

Dendahl, Alice   147

Denver   5, 14, 15, 22, 26, 27, 31, 35, 43, 113

Denver Olympic Committee   113-115

Denver Post Jumping Program   81

Denver, University of   103, 106

de Pret, Count Phillipe   47

Dercum, Edna   79, 99, 147

Dercum, Max   79, 99, 147

Dercum, Rolf   79, 147

Dercum, Sunni   79

Devecka, Mike   147

Devereaux, W. B.   17

Devil's Hangover   166

Devil's Thumb   166

Dillon   26, 80, 95, 166

Dole, Minot   57, 147

Duchin, Eddie   37

Duke, H. Benjamin Jr.   147

Duncan, J. J. Jr.   53, 147

Duncan, Ray   99, 147

Durango   86, 103, 106

Durrance, Dick   48, 51, 70, 73, 74, 79, 147

Durrance, Dick Jr.   74

Dwyer, Charles   131, 147

Dyer, John   9, 12, 13, 148

Eagle   119

Eaton, Earl V.   89, 148

Eaton, Gordi   106

Eaton, Margaret   148

Eflin, Dick   91, 148

Eldora   166

Elisha, Lawrence   81, 148

Elisha, M. J.   106, 148

Ellefsen, Didrik   148

Elliot, Jere   84, 148

Elliot, Jon   84, 148

Elliot, Mike   148

Emerald Mountain   166

Engel, Ernst   148

Engel, George   148

Engren, Karle   52, 148

Equitable Family Ski Challenge   171

Eriksen, Stein   74, 96, 133, 148

Eskimo Club   39, 171

Esmiol, Merritt   148

Estes Park   31, 53, 89, 165

Evans, Roger   148

Evergreen   185, 113 166

Fairfield-Smith   148

Fairplay   9, 12

Farwell, Ted   148

Faulkenberg, Jinx   62

Fawn Valley   101, 66

Federation Internationale De Ski   74, 171

Ferguson, Ian   148

Fern & Odessa Lakes   31

Ferno, Mike   52

Ferries-Arroyo, Barbara   106, 148

Fetcher, John   96, 148

Finlandia Trophy   171

Finnegan, Frank   26

First of Denver Cup   172

Fiske, Billy   49, 58, 149

Flood, Eyvind   27, 149

Floystad, Oyvind   149

Flynn, Tom J.   47, 49, 149

Ford, Gerald R.   91, 93, 117

Ford, Grant   149

Ford, Mark   149

Forest Lakes   86, 166

Forest Service, U. S.   48, 53, 69, 113, 121, 123, 131

Fort Carson   63

Fort Lewis College   106, 111

Fort Lewis, Washington   58

Foster, Bill   149

Fowler, Donald   149

Frame, Bill & Mary   149

Franconia, N. H.   5

Fraser Valley   166

Frisco   26

Froelicher, Charles   116, 149

Frosty Basin   166

Fun Valley   85, 166

Gallagher, Mike   149

Galstead Memorial Award   172

Gardiner, Charles F.   15

Garland, Earl   149

Geier, Hans   149

Gelande   172

Genesee Mountain   27, 29, 31, 55, 166

Geneva Basin   166

Gibbons, James   13, 149

Glen Cove   53, 55, 84, 166

Glenwood Springs   43, 53, 100

Glenwood Mountain Park   166

Golden   119

Golden Horn Restaurant   65, 73

Golden Quill Award   172

Goliad Oil   119

Gorsuch, Dave   83, 149

Gorsuch, George   149

Gorsuch, Jack   83, 149

Gramshammer, Pepi   149

Grand Junction   55

Grand Lake   53

Grand Mesa   55, 99

Grand Prix Du Megeve   97, 172

Grant, Bill   149

Grant, Edwin   149

Grant, Neil   32, 149

Gray, Bob   150

Grazier, Mike   150

Groswald, Gerald   96, 150

Groswald, Thor   34, 39, 40, 47, 63, 79, 83, 111, 150

Guanella Pass   119

Gunnison   4, 7, 15, 18, 43, 47

Gunnison Snowshoe Club   17   .

Hackney, Edgar   150

Haemerle, Florian   34, 150

Hahnenkamm Races   172

Hahn's Peak   119

Hale, Camp see Camp Hale

Hale, Irving   58

Hall, Henry   150

Halstead Award   172

Hammerness, Odd   75

Hannah, Joan   150

Hansen, Hans   150

Hansen, Ole-Ivar   75

Harriman, Averell   5, 37

Harriman Cup   97, 172

Harsh, James L.   53, 103, 150

Hart, Gary   117

Hastings, James K.   15

Hastings, Merrill   65

Haugen, Anders   4, 5, 26, 31, 150

Haugen, Lars   5, 26, 31, 150

Hauk, Paul   124, 133, 150

Hayden   103

Hayes, Maj. Gen. George P.   63, 150

Head, Howard   150

Heron, Robert & Kenneth   80, 150

Hesperus   119, 167

Heuga, Jim   74, 106

Hidden Park 85

Hidden Valley 89, 167

Hideway Park 85, 167

Higgs, John 151

Highland Bavarian Lodge 49

Hilton, Conrad 69, 150

Hinderman, Tim 107, 151

Hinkley, Don 151

Hirsch Award 172

Hitchcock, Peter 151

Hlavata, Jana 151

Hodges, Bill & Joe 151

Hoeschler, Jim 106

Holden, John 151

Holliday Hill 100, 167

Holmen-Jensen, Tom 151

Holmenkollen 4, 21, 172

Holmenkollen-Kandahar 172

Homewood Park 32, 167

Hossier Pass 52

Horiuche, Harold 151

Hosberg, Jim 151

Hot Sulphur Springs 22, 53, 65, 84, 103, 139, 167

Howard, Menefree 31, 151

Howelsen, Carl 19, 21, 22, 23, 25, 27, 31, 83, 139, 151

Howelsen Hill 25, 55, 65, 167

Howelsen, Lief 27

Huddleston, Sam 96, 151

Hudspeth, Jim 151

Hughes, Berrian 40, 151

Hunter's Pass 18

Huntington, Sam 151

Idledale 54

Idlewild 119, 167

Independence Pass 17

Indianhead Mountain 85, 167

International Ski Racers Association 172

International Speed Skiing Association 172

Irwin 15, 138

Iselin, Fred 73, 151

Ishpeming, Michigan 4

Jacobs, Tom 106, 151

Jackson, Bob 115

Jankovsky, Joe 151

Janss Corporation 96

Janss, William 52, 96, 151

Jansen, Erik 151

Jay, John 59, 62, 65, 151

Jeffers Cup 41, 172

Jencks, Moses Amos 47, 152

Jerome Hotel 61, 70

Johnson, Albert 15, 152

Johnstone, Robert C. 152

Jones, Greg 152

Jones, Mark 152

Jones Pass 40, 167

Jones, "Whip" 75, 95, 152

Judd, William R. 152

Juhan, Joe 152

Jumbo Run 167

Jump, Larry 59, 65, 79, 81, 152

Jump, Marnie 81, 152

Junior Races 172

Kandahar   41, 172

Kane, Jim   152

Kashiwa, Hank   152

Kebler Pass   15

Kendall, Bob   152

Kendall Mountain   85, 167

Kendrick, Charles   152

Kendrick, Jack   32, 37, 43, 152

Keystone   79, 99, 138, 167

Kiandra Ski Club   3

Kidd, William "Billy"   152

Kidder, Arthur   152

Kidder-Lee, Barbara   70, 152

Kinney, Mark   152

Klumb, Larry   152

Knowlton, Steve   59, 65, 73, 74, 89, 121, 153

Koch, Bill   153

Krog, George   153

Kuss, Adolph   111, 153

Lafferty, Mike   153

Lake Catamount   167

Lake City   167

Lake Placid, New York   5

Lake, Rial   47, 153

Lamunyan, Ed   153

Lang, Oho   153

Lance Cup   172

Lange, Robert B.   153

La Porte, California   3

Larkin, James R. "Gus"   153

Larsh, Don   83, 153

Lauberhorn   172

Lawrence, Andrea (Mead)   74, 153

Lawrence, David   74, 153

Layman Trophy   172

Leadville   9, 14, 26, 55, 59, 60, 95, 103

Letson, Ed   153

Levy, Lynn   153

Lewis, Charles D.   115, 153

Ling Temco Voght (LTV)   99

Litchfield, Johnny   64, 71, 73, 153

Little, Rogers   153

Livingston, Lou   153

Lodders, Georgia   121, 154

L'Orange, John   154

Loveland Basin   89, 167

Loveland Pass   5, 15, 39, 40, 79

Lynch, Kerry   153

MacLennan, Kenneth   111, 154

Mace, Stewart   154

Madigan, Mike   154

Magnifico, Mike   154

Mahoney, Billy   154

Malin, Jeff   154

Marolt, Bill   74, 106, 107, 154

Marolt, Bud   154

Marble   119, 124, 167

Marcy Expedition   7

Marshall, Gen. George   57

Marshall, Jack   154

Marshall Pass   47

Martin, Todd   121, 154

Martin-Kuntz, Marti   154

Mary Jane Run 167

Masbruch, Evelyn 154

Master Ski Series 172

Matis, Clark 154

Matt, Toni 51, 59, 65, 154

May Company 36, 39

Maynard, Robert 154

McCoy, Dennis 154

McDermott, Wes 47, 154

McDonald, Otto 19, 154

McGill, Tim 154

McGowan, Graeme 29, 32, 79, 154

McGrane, Dennis 155

McKinney, Steve 155

McLean, Robert "Barney" 52, 53, 65, 70, 155

McMurtry, John 155

McNeil, Chris 84

McReady, John 155

Meadow Mountain 167

Merrill, Hollis 26, 155

Merrill, Marcellus 26, 83, 155

Mesa College 103

Mesa Creek 164

Meyers, Charlie 155

Michaelson's Ranch 167

Mill, Andy 155

Miller, Dwight 155

Miller, Earnest 155

Miller, Jim 155

Miller, Mack 155

Miller, Warren 155

Mills, Enos C. 15, 155

Milstein, Richard 120, 155

Mitchell, R. Garrett 121, 155

Mize, Dick 155

Moffat Tunnel 32

Molterer, Anderl 155

Monarch 52, 83, 167

Monson, D. 53, 156

Montezuma Basin 15, 119

Morris, John 156

Mosquito Pass 9, 12

Moulton, William 156

Mount Crested Butte, Town of 93

Mount Sneffles Snowshoe Club 17

Mount Werner 97, 99

Murri, Robert 156

Nathan, A. F. 17

National Collegiate Athletic Association 103, 107, 173

National Ski Areas Association 173

National Ski Association 57, 106

National Ski Championships 173

National Ski Hall of Fame 4, 28, 103

National Ski Patrol 103, 173

National Ski Trail 135

National Standard Ski Race (NASTAR) 106, 173

National Veterans' Race 173

Navarre Restaurant 37

Neusteter, Myron 57, 156

Nevins, Hugh J. 156

Nielson, Don 156

Nilsen, Egil 156

Nilsgard, Vidar 156

Nilson, Swan   14, 156

Nitze, Paul   69, 75, 156

Nitze, William A.   67

Norheim, Sondrie   5

North Peak   168

Norwegian Snowshoes   3

Obermeyer, Klaus   156

Ohio Pass   15

Old Sam   168

O'Leary, Hal   156

Olson, Willis   156

Olympics, Winter   26, 49, 64, 83, 97, 106, 113-115, 173

Omtvedt, Ragner   4, 25, 156

Opaas, Kjetil   156

Operation Ski Jump   63

Ormes, Robert M.   156

Oro City   9, 12

Otero College   103

Ouray   13, 17, 86, 168

Outing Magazine   4, 17

Overland, Terje   156

Paepcke, Elizabeth   51, 60, 64, 156

Paepcke, Walter   51, 67, 69, 70, 73, 75, 156

Pandero   168

Pando   57, 58

Panion, Paul   93, 156

Parent, Alec   156

Parker, Robert W.   59, 65, 90, 117, 121, 157

Patterson, William   157

Peaceful Valley   65, 168

Pearl Pass   48

Pearson, Dale   157

Pederson, Olav   157

Peet, Barney   157

Pejak, Sharon   74

Perchlick, Dick   157

Perry, Henry   157

Perry, Marjorie   22, 32, 157

Perry, Robert   157

Peary-Smith, Crosby   65, 83, 157

Pesman, Jerry   157

Peterson, Dick   99, 157

Pew, Bill   157

Pfeifer, Freidl   41, 59, 63, 64, 67, 68, 75, 157

Phelps, Ken   157

Phipps, Allan   157

Pikes Peak   119, 168

Pikes Peak Ski Club   53

Pioneer   43, 48, 130, 168

Pitcher, Bill K.   157

Poma Lifts   81

Porcarelli, Mike   159

Porcupine Gulch   39, 169

Powderhorn   65, 99, 168

Praeger, Walter   59, 65, 157

Prendergast, James   93, 157

Prestrud Jump   26, 168

Prestrud, Peter   26, 83, 157

Professional Skier of the Year Award   173

Pueblo College   103

Purgatory   99, 168

Pyles, Rudd   83, 157

Pyles, Scott   83, 157

Pytte, Peter   157

Quick's Hill   47, 168

Ranchetto, Paul   158

Rahm, John   95, 158

Ralston, Norman   31, 158

Ralston-Purina   99

Rand, Jay   158

Raton-Sugarite   86, 168

Red Mountain (Georgetown)   40

Red Mountain (Glenwood Springs)   43, 53, 100, 168

Red Mountain (Ouray)   168

Red Onion Saloon   65, 73

Red Wing, Minnesota   4

Regis College   103

Reilly, Barney   31, 158

Reischl, Steve   158

Rice, Fred   91

Richardson, Tom   158

Rideout, Percy   158

Riggs, John   101

Riiber, Harold   158

Rilliet Hill   31, 168

Rimrock   168

Roaring Fork Ski Club   50

Roberts, Curtis   158

Robinson, Edith   71, 158

Robinson, Vernon   158

Roch, Andre   50, 70, 158

Roch Cup   70, 97, 173

Rockefeller, J. R.   158

Rocky Mountain Intercollegiate Association   173

Rocky Mountain National Park   15, 31

Rocky Mountain Ski Association   36, 173

Rocky Mountain News Ski School   80

Rodolph, Katy   84, 158

Rogers, James Grafton   158

Rolfe, Col. Onslow   62, 63, 158

Rollins Pass   85, 168

Romine, Mike   106, 158

Ronnestad, Oddvar   158

Ross, Harold   62

Rounds, Bill   95, 159

Rowen, Robert   50, 159

Rowland, Harold "Red"   70, 95, 159

Rozman Hill   48, 168

Ronnette, Evelyn   41, 159

Russell, Bob   159

Ryan, Ted   50, 58, 159

Sabich, Vladimir "Spider"   159

Sabin, Mary S.   159

Sagebrush Hill   168

Salida   47, 52, 137

San Isabel   168

Sattersum, John   159

Sayer, J. E.   53, 159

Sayer, William   96

Sayre, Robert   159

Schaeffler, Willy   81, 107-109, 159

Schauffler, Fred

Schmidt, Agnell   22, 159

Schnackenberg, Karl   159

Schnackenberg, Rodolph   59, 65, 84, 159

Schneibs, Otto   134, 148, 159

Schneider, Hannes   4, 59, 159

Schobinger, Charles W.   160

Schoenberger Award   173

Schoenberger, Dick   160

Schweitzer, Charles   47, 160

Scott, Bob   160

Seibert, Peter   59, 65, 89, 90, 160

Selback, Chris   160

Sevold, Clarence   160

Seven Utes   168

Severson, Sue & Daughter   160

Sharktooth   119, 168

Sharp, W. Edward   160

Shick, Ellen   160

Shrine Pass   64

Silver Belt Trophy   173

Silver Creek   119, 168

Silver Hills   168

Silverstein, Pete   160

Silver Tip Ranch   168

Silverton   14, 55, 85, 169

Simon, Tom   160

Simonton, Donald   121

Ski Magazine   65

Ski Tip Ranch   79, 99

Ski Trail Mountain   169

Ski Writer's Award   173

Skiing Magazine   90

Skimeister Award   173

Small, Allen   100, 160

Smith, Dudley   160

Smith, Margaret   160

Snobble, Jack   160

Snodgrass Mountain   124, 169

Snow King   169

Snowmass   65, 70, 96

Sorensen, Harald "Pop"   59, 65, 81, 161

Southern Rocky Mountain Ski Association   41, 121, 173

Spar Gulch Trail   71

Spence, Gale "Spider"   160

Spencer, Alison Owen   160

Squaw Pass   85, 169

St. Mary's Glacier   48, 52, 55, 169

Stagecoach   119, 169

Stallard House   121

Staub, Roger   160

Steamboat Lake   119, 169

Steamboat Ski Area   169

Steamboat Springs   15, 22, 23, 26, 27, 28, 29, 55, 83, 96, 103, 113, 139

Steele, John   29, 83, 123, 160

Stefansson, Vilhjamer   62

Stevens, Charles P.   160

Stillman, Richard   160

Stoner   86, 119, 169

Storm Mountain   84, 96, 97, 169

Sudler, Amos   32, 160

Sugar Bowl, California   5

Sun Valley, Idaho   5, 37, 41, 67, 73

Sunlight   101, 169

Sunrise Peak Tramway   130

Suttle, Mrs.   15, 161

Swenson, Henry   161

Tagert, Billy   161

Tammarron   55, 100, 103, 169

Taylor, Clif   161

Taylor, Dick   161

Taylor, Edward F.   70, 101

Telluride   13, 55, 103, 116, 169

Temple, Jeff   161

Temple, Jim   84, 96, 161

Tenderfoot Mountain (Cripple Creek)   169

Tenderfoot Mountain (Gunnison)   17, 169

Tennessee Pass   57, 64

Tenth Mountain Division   57-65, 68, 71

Tenth Mountain Trail Association   135

Thomas, Lowell   5, 161

Thompkins, Dick   36, 39, 161

Thompson, Josh   161

Thompson, "Snowshoe"   3

Tin Cup   48

Top o' La Veta   85, 169

Torkle, Torgel   59, 63, 161

Trap Door Lodge   37

Tread of Pioneer's Museum   121

Trinidad College   103

Tschudi, Otto   161

Twentieth Century Fox   95

Twin Sisters   169

Upham, Tom   161

U.S. Ski Association   4

U.S. Ski Patrol   57

Vail   64, 89, 90, 93, 113, 117, 119, 121, 138, 169

Vail Cup   174

Vaille, Agnes   161

Vaille, Lucretia   32, 161

Valentine, Don   161

Valkama, Aarne   161

Vanatta, Lonny   84, 161

Vanderhodf, John   100, 117, 161

Vasquez   169

Veterans' Races, see National Veteran's Races

Victor   5

Viking Division   57

Vilhjamer, Dr.   30

Vincellette, Alf   162

W Mountain   17

Wadsworth, Stan   162

Waldrop, A. Gayle   162

Walker, Gladys, see Werner, Gladys

Walton, Ralph   93, 162

Wegeman, Al   29, 83, 162

Wegeman, Katy (Randolph)   162

Wegeman, Keith   83, 162

Wegeman, Paul   83, 162

Welch, Tom   93, 162

Werner Award   174

Werner, Mount   97, 99, 169

Werner, Gladys "Skeeter"   84, 162

Werner, Loris   84, 162

Werner, Wallace "Buddy"   84, 96, 97, 99, 106, 162